Religious Courts in the Jurisprudence of the European Court of Human Rights

Law and Religion

Volumes published in this Brill Research Perspectives title are listed at *brill.com/rplr*

Religious Courts in the Jurisprudence of the European Court of Human Rights

By

Michał Rynkowski

For Joanna and Emilia

BRILL

LEIDEN | BOSTON

This paperback book edition is simultaneously published as issue 2.1 (2019) of *Law and Region*, DOI:10.1163/24682993-12340005.

Library of Congress Control Number: 2019946480

Typeface for the Latin, Greek, and Cyrillic scripts: "Brill". See and download: brill.com/brill-typeface.

ISBN 978-90-04-41648-2 (paperback)
ISBN 978-90-04-41650-5 (e-book)

Religious Courts in the Jurisprudence of the European Court of Human Rights

By

Michał Rynkowski

For Joanna and Emilia

BRILL

LEIDEN | BOSTON

This paperback book edition is simultaneously published as issue 2.1 (2019) of *Law and Region*, DOI:10.1163/24682993-12340005.

Library of Congress Control Number: 2019946480

Typeface for the Latin, Greek, and Cyrillic scripts: "Brill". See and download: brill.com/brill-typeface.

ISBN 978-90-04-41648-2 (paperback)
ISBN 978-90-04-41650-5 (e-book)

This book is printed on acid-free paper and produced in a sustainable manner.

Contents

Religious Courts in the Jurisprudence of the European Court of Human Rights

Michał Rynkowski
michal.rynkowski@yahoo.com

Abstract

Religious courts have for centuries been part of the European legal landscape. Almost all churches and religious communities have their own judicial systems, often composed of courts or tribunals ordered hierarchically. The aim of this paper is to present cases from the jurisprudence of the European Court of Human Rights, in which a religious court was involved at the stage of domestic proceedings. The twelve cases in question originate from a number of European States, from Italy to Finland and from the UK to Turkey—and in one particular case, Israel. The applicants belonged to many denominations, predominantly Christian. The Court of Human Rights (and before that, the Commission of Human Rights) has been concerned, in the main, with religious courts in terms of compliance with the requirement for a fair hearing by an independent and impartial tribunal under Article 6 of the European Convention of Human Rights. The Court has come to various conclusions—for example, it accepted that courts of the Church of England comply with the requirement, it questioned whether the cathedral chapter of the Evangelical-Lutheran Church in Finland did so, and it indirectly criticized proceedings before the Roman Rota of the Catholic Church. The most recent judgment from September 2017, *Nagy v. Hungary*, and in particular many associated dissenting opinions, demonstrate that the matter is worthy of study, particularly in the contemporary context of religious freedom. Nevertheless, the cases are so different that it is difficult to discern a coherent line of jurisprudence, and the Court itself hardly ever refers to its own previous judgments in this field.

Keywords

religious courts – European Court of Human Rights – freedom of religion – fair trial – independent tribunal

 | DOI:10.1163/9789004416505_002

1 Introduction

1.1 *Background: The Religious Courts at a Glance*

Religious courts are a fascinating topic for research. Their history is usually counted in centuries,[1] and their existence is confirmed in the earliest sacred scriptures.[2] Over the course of centuries, they became institutionally separate and therefore quite distinct from state courts.[3] Nevertheless, as with state courts, most religious courts form complicated hierarchical systems in terms of subject-matter and appellate jurisdiction.[4] N. Doe sees hierarchical judicial structures as one of the principles of law common to Christian Churches.[5]

However, in Europe, the precise juridical status of religious courts depends on two factors: the state in which they function; and the denomination to which they belong. On the one hand, with regard to the State, the legal framework relating to religious courts reflects to a major extent the legal *status quo* and legal philosophy underlying state-church relations in Europe.[6] For example, in Italy, judgments of Catholic courts in matrimonial cases, if they undergo a special procedure of *delibazione*, which provides for recognition of

---

1 Ecclesiastical and state courts existed at the time of the emperor Constantine the Great in the 4th century AD: E.L. Richter, R.W. Dove, and W. Kahl (eds.), *Lehrbuch des katholischen und evangelischen Kirchenrechts*, ed. 8, 1886 (§206, p. 742).

2 See e.g. for Jewish judicial bodies, L. Panafit, 'Juridiction religieuse: Judaïsme', in: F. Messner (ed.), *Dictionnaire Droit des Religions*, Paris, 2010, p. 430. Judges and courts are mentioned in the Book of Deuteronomy.

3 E.g. for England in the twelfth century, see R. Sandberg, *Law and Religion*, Cambridge 2014, p. 20.

4 This is so for the most common systems of religious courts, e.g. the Catholic, Lutheran or Church of England. See also the comparative study in N. Doe, *Christian Law: Contemporary Principles*, Cambridge 2013, p. 164. A number of interesting detailed reports was gathered as a result of the meeting of the *Interfaith Legal Advisers Network*, Lambeth Palace, London, in January 2009; http://www.law.cf.ac.uk/clr/networks/ilan6.html, accessed on 9.05.2019.

5 N. Doe, *Christian Law*, op. cit., p. 392, principle 23: Church courts and tribunals; The *Statement of Principles of Christian Law*, Rome 2016, 19 *Ecclesiastical Law Journal* (2017), 138–155 (Section V).

6 Throughout Europe, there are three basic models of the state-church research: strict separation (France, Slovenia); cooperation between State and Church (Germany, Italy); and links between Church and State (UK, Greece, Denmark). Probably the most comprehensive overview of the Church-State relations available is: G. Robbers (ed.), *State and Church in the EU*, Baden-Baden 2005 (the third edition is being prepared for 2019), more recently in the *Encyclopedia of Law and Religion*, G. Robbers, and W. Cole Durham Jr. (eds.). Leiden and Boston 2016. A thematic overview is offered by N. Doe in *Law and Religion in Europe: A Comparative Introduction*, Oxford 2011.

ecclesiastical judgments by the Italian state courts, as prescribed by state law,[7] are treated like judgments of foreign courts and are enforceable according to state law. In Germany, the existence and functioning of Catholic courts is understood by the State as a part of the exercise of autonomy by Churches and religious communities, as enshrined in the German Basic Law (and more precisely, the *Weimarer Reichsverfassung* 1919, which is still in force under Article 140 of the current *Grundgesetz*); however, there is no direct recognition of their judgments, and certainly not in matrimonial cases. In France, the State does not recognise the existence of religious courts and basically ignores their jurisprudence. This is discussed more fully below in section 2 below which seeks to classify European countries into five groups.

On the other hand, with regard to denomination, within a country, the religious courts of one denomination may have a status different from those of other denominations in that country. For example, the courts of the Church of England are public courts in England, while courts of other churches and religious communities are private *fora*, but may also be treated as arbitration bodies provided they fulfil certain conditions.[8] Similarly, in Italy, Catholic courts enjoy a status in civil law which cannot be compared with that of other religious courts, as seen in section 4.

Moreover, the courts of different denominations handle different cases: while Catholic courts are predominantly preoccupied with marriage cases (more precisely, with nullity), a good number of cases of the Evangelical Church in Germany, EKD,[9] relate to the labour conditions and the legal status of clergy (in particular dismissal cases, the so-called *Statusklagen*); and the diocesan consistory courts of the Church of England deal with cases which concern consecrated property and the issuing of faculties to authorise work on or in them which affects the fabric and contents of church buildings and their churchyards (e.g. exhumation of human remains).[10]

With regard to terminology, whilst the expression "ecclesiastical court" may be familiar to readers, and this term is appropriate when used in relation to the courts of Christians, in so far as this study also deals with the judicial bodies

7 F. Finocchiaro, *Diritto ecclesiastico*, Bologna 2003, p. 330, extensively discussed in the case of Pellegrini, see below.

8 UK Arbitration Act 1996: https://www.legislation.gov.uk/ukpga/1996/23, accessed 22.3.2018.

9 The *Evangelische Kirche in Deutschland* is a pan-German association of Lutheran, Reformed and United Churches, www.ekd.de. The structure of the EKD courts and of the courts of other churches and religious communities is presented below in part 2.

10 A. McGregor, 'Religion, Doctrine and Ecclesiastical Courts', 13 *Ecclesiastical Law Journal* (2011), 333.

of other religions (e.g. Beth Din in Judaism), the term "religious court" is used throughout this study as a more appropriate, inclusive term.

Finally, this study is based on research undertaken over ten years. Following the growing awareness of data protection, more and more data is anonymized,[11] although the judgments of the ECtHR still bear the names derived from the name of the applicant. Therefore, individuals' names are omitted unless they appear in the database of the ECtHR and in literature.

1.2 *The Case Law of the ECtHR*

The European Commission of Human Rights (until 1998) and the European Court of Human Rights (hereafter ECtHR) in Strasbourg, among thousands of judgments and decisions, have issued several hundred judgments and decisions relating to freedom of religion.[12] These cases concern various important issue, such as: the obligation to indicate religious affiliation on official documents; religious objections to compulsory military service; and the right to wear religious garments or symbols. Some relate to the autonomy of churches and religious communities, which in itself was a subject of much academic study at the beginning of this century.[13] Within this limited group of judgments, only a very small number concern, directly or indirectly, religious courts.

For the purposes of this study, these cases are divided into two broad groups, considered in sections 3 and 4, namely:

1) cases in which:
   - religious courts are treated on the margins of the case or where they were not a part of the procedure, although *prima facie* it seems that they would have been the appropriate institutions to adjudicate;
   - the autonomy of churches and religious communities was discussed, whereas—implicitly—church autonomy should be understood as a guarantee for the existence and proper functioning of religious courts;
   - the ECtHR and state courts in the domestic process cite the internal law of churches and religious communities, which underlines the legal character of internal religious norms, being the foundations of ecclesiastical/religious jurisprudence; and:

---

11 E.g. the German translation of the decision relating to application 39775/04 mentions Mr. R., born in 19 … and living in M., while the French text still reads: Roland Reuter, born in 1955, living in Moers.

12 http://www.echr.coe.int/Documents/Guide_Art_9_ENG.pdf, overview from 2015, accessed on 21.02.2018. Legally speaking, only around 40 judgments have been issued thus far, remainder were declared as inadmissible.

13 H. Warnink (ed.), *Legal Position of Churches and Church Autonomy*, Leuven, 2001; G. Robbers (ed.), *Church Autonomy: A Comparative Survey*, Frankfurt, 2001.

2) in twelve cases, the process in the religious court constituted a part of the domestic procedure, before a complaint was lodged with the European Court of Human Rights, and where that court had to make a decision on the proceedings before such a religious court (section 4).

1.3 *Cases Seen from Different Perspectives*

The twelve cases presented in section 4 are not well-known. Typing the names of the applicants yields very few hits on the internet and very few academic papers.[14] The books and commentaries referring to Article 9 of ECHR (and to Article 10 of the EU Charter of Fundamental Rights) do not list them as leading or important cases of the ECtHR.[15] Some cases are mentioned in the overview of the Court's jurisprudence on ECHR Articles 6 and 9, which are periodically updated and published on the website of the Court.[16] The twelve cases are also absent from a factsheet on freedom of religion, published by the Court (most recently in June 2017). Moreover, although the ECtHR usually refers in its judgments to previous cases, this is not (or very rarely) so in our twelve cases—it is almost as if the ECtHR seeks to avoid making public its decisions in this field. In addition, the judgments presented here are usually available only in the language of the proceedings in question, or both in English and in French—they are rarely translated into other languages (all translations in other languages are duly noted in this study). Last but not least, the judgments in question have not attracted much attention—unlike some very well-known cases, such as *Lautsi v. Italy*,[17] where nine states intervened (Bulgaria, Cyprus, the Russian

14 This paper is based on one of the chapters of the book of M. Rynkowski, *Sądy wyznaniowe we współczesnym europejskim porządku prawnym* [Religious courts in the European contemporary legal system], Wrocław 2013, as an updated and reworked version. The only text in English on the subject is a short text also by M. Rynkowski, 'Religious Courts in the Jurisprudence of the European Court of Human Rights', *Ecclesiastical Law Journal*, volume 18, issue 1 (January 2016), pp. 62–66, doi: 10.1017/S0956618X15000848.

15 R. McCrea. 'Art. 10 [of the Charter] Freedom of Thought, Conscience and Religion [with extensive references to the judgments of the ECtHR]', in: S. Peers, T. Hervey, J. Kenner, and A. Ward (eds.), *The EU Charter of fundamental rights*, Oxford and Portland 2014; also: H.-W. Rengeling, and P. Szczekalla (eds.), *Grundrechte in der Europäischen Union, Charta der Grundrechte und Allgemeine Rechtsgrundsätze*, Köln 2004, also with extensive lists of the ECtHR judgments.

16 See footnote number 1.

17 Appl. 30814/06, judgment: of the Grand Chamber of 18.03.2011, available in English and French and translated into 19 other languages. See also: R. Torfs, 'The presence of the cross in public spaces from the perspective of the European Court of Human Rights', in P. Stanisz, M. Zawiślak, and M. Ordon (eds.), *The Presence of the Cross in Public Spaces*, Cambridge 2016, p. 11.

Federation, Greece, Lithuania, Malta, Monaco, Romania and the Republic of San Marino), and which was later translated by the Court into many languages.

The cases presented in section 4 seem to be very different: the applicants were a Dane, an Englishman, three Finns, a Greek, an Italian, a Slovak, two Germans, a Turkish-Frenchwoman (a person with dual citizenship) and a Hungarian. They belonged to different denominations—two Catholics, an Orthodox, an Anglican, five Lutherans, a Reformed, a Jew, and a woman of unspecified religion with a case before a rabbinical court in Israel. Such a variety of applicants might be understood to represent well the make-up of modern European societies, save for the absence of Muslims and Jehovah's Witnesses.[18] Applicants also differ in their status and profession—among them were eight priests, a church assistant (a verger, Mr. Helle), a man and two women of unknown professions (respectively, Mr. Kohn, Ms. Pellegrini and Ms. Eskinazi).

The subjects of the complaints were also different. These cases concerned:

- disciplinary proceedings as to a suspension or transfer of a priest to another parish (*X v. Denmark*, *Skordas*, *Šupa*, *Ahtinen*, *Launikari*, *Reuter*, *Nagy*), or against a priest accused of adultery (*Tyler*);
- issues related to the social insurance of a verger (*Helle*);
- difficulties in proceedings before Catholic church courts and then before Italian state courts (*Pellegrini*);
- the issue related to premises occupied by a religious association (*Kohn*);
- matters relating to parental rights (*Eskinazi*).

Interestingly, the applicants based their complaints on a range of Articles in the ECHR. Most referred to Articles 6 (fair trial—*Tyler*, *Helle*, *Ahtinen*, *Pellegrini*, *Reuter*—or the length of the procedure—*Launikari*) and 9 (freedom of religion), often combined with other Articles (Articles 6 and 8 in *Eskinazi*, Articles 6 and 3 in *Kohn*, and Articles 6 and 13 in *Supa*). However, some applicants also invoked other Articles, including Articles 3 and 4 (*Skordas*: here the application was based on violation of Art. 3, 4 and 9).

The element which links all these cases is the fact that before a complaint was lodged with the European Court of Human Rights—and before that with its predecessor, the European Commission of Human Rights—a religious court was involved at an earlier stage. These cases originate primarily from countries where the church is strongly associated with the state, both formally (UK, Greece) and informally (Germany, Finland, Italy, Slovakia).

---

18 See e.g. the Muslim Arbitration Tribunal in the UK; http://www.matribunal.com. Other Muslim courts, mainly known as shariah councils, have hardly any links to state courts and so lack the links required for a case to reach the ECtHR.

The courts in question are:

- a consistory court of the Danish *Folkekirke*, or rather of the Danish Ministry of Church Affairs;
- a diocesan court of the Church of England (consistory court);
- a cathedral chapter of the Evangelical Lutheran Church of Finland (in three cases, *Helle, Launikari* and *Ahtinen*);
- a court of the Orthodox diocese of Nea Smirni in Greece;
- a (Catholic) church court of the Lazio region and in the second instance the Roman Rota;
- the Supreme Court of the Apostolic Signature (Vatican City, or, rather, the Holy See);
- an arbitration and administration court at the Central Council of Jews in Germany;
- a rabbinical court in Tel-Aviv (Batei Hadîn Harabaniim Haezori);
- two instances of courts of the Evangelical Church (*Verwaltungskammer der Evangelischen Kirche im Rheinland* and the *Verwaltungsgerichtshof der Evangelischen Kirche der Union*);
- a first-instance and second-instance ecclesiastical court of the Reformed Church of Hungary.

In two cases (*Pellegrini* and *Šupa*), there is a reference to previous judgments of the highest Catholic courts, namely the Roman Rota and the Supreme Tribunal of the Apostolic Signature. Although their offices are physically based in Rome, they belong to the judiciary of the Holy See. This element further complicates the legal situation, since neither the Holy See nor the State of Vatican City are parties to the Convention.[19] Declaring the jurisprudence of these church courts—even indirectly—as inconsistent with ECHR principles could lead to international misunderstandings. As will be seen below, on a small number of occasions the Court avoided in an elegant manner treating this matter, claiming either non-exhaustion of the domestic procedure or that being a priest is not a right under Article 6 of the Convention.

As seen above, the legal standing of a religious court depends of two factors: the state and the denomination in which that court operates. On the basis of these two factors, the European Court of Human Rights has:

- recognised that a court (of the Church of England) was an impartial court within the meaning of Article 6 of the European Convention (*Tyler*);
- recognised that the cathedral chapter of the Evangelical Lutheran Church of Finland (ELCF) was a body closely linked to the relevant employer,

19 Canon 1404 of the Code of Canon Law, "Prima Sedes a nemine judicatur"—Nobody can judge the First Seat (i.e. the Holy See)—is given sometimes as a justification.

because a bishop was *ex officio* chair of the cathedral chapter (*Helle*). The ECtHR underlined, however, that the relevant appeal body is the Finnish Supreme Administrative Court, which fully complies with the requirements of Article 6. A few years later, in the case of a parish priest (*Ahtinen*), also before the cathedral chapter of the ELCF, the ECtHR avoided addressing this matter, see below;
- held that the decisions of the courts of the Greek Orthodox Church are not subject to review by state courts (*Skordas*);[20]
- criticised indirectly the proceedings before the courts of the Catholic Church, including that of the Roman Rota (Pellegrini);
- where the Slovakian state courts referred to the canon law and jurisprudence of the (Catholic) Supreme Tribunal of the Apostolic Signature, held that the time had passed for submitting the complaint, so that the application was inadmissible, without commenting on the merits (*Šupa*);
- not questioned the competence (and thus the jurisdiction) of the arbitration and administrative courts at the Central Council of Jews (*Zentraler Judenrat*) in Germany, or the rabbinical courts of Israel (respectively, *Kohn* and *Eskinazi*);
- tacitly agreed that the ecclesiastical courts are solely competent (*Reuter*);
- recognised that the State courts may define the jurisdiction of religious courts, not the religious courts themselves (*Nagy*), however an important question was raised by a number of judges in their dissenting opinion, whether a citizen, who pays taxes [to the state], can be deprived of a right to a [state] trial;
- declined to comment answer on the role of the consistory court of the Danish National Church (*X v. Denmark*).

Last but not least, it should be emphasized that with the exception of *X v. Denmark* (1976), all the cases discussed in this study were adjudged during the last years of the 20th century or in the first years of the 21st century (*Tyler* 1993, *Helle* 1997, *Skordas* 2000, Kohn 2000, *Launikari* 2000, Pellegrini 2001, *Eskinazi* 2005, *Šupa* 2007, *Ahtinen* 2008, *Reuter* 2011). Particularly busy were the years 2000 and 2001, when four decisions and judgments were issued. Hence, religious courts represent a relatively new focus for Strasbourg jurisprudence, with the very interesting judgment (and dissenting opinions) of *Károly Nagy v. Hungary*, issued on 14 September 2017, as the most recent.

20 This statement seems to be simplistic and not very plausible—even in the same case of *Skordas*, the State authorities assessed and quashed the decisions of Orthodox Church authorities.

This study does not discuss in detail cases in which the ECtHR commented on church autonomy, though they are briefly mentioned in section 3 below. Such cases are presented in section 4 only if a religious court was involved in the domestic procedure (e.g. as in *Kohn*).

1.4 *No Cross-references to Previous ECtHR Cases and Other Technical Matters*

As seen above, although as a matter of practice the ECtHR usually extensively refers to its own earlier judgments and jurisprudence, in the matter of religious courts the ECtHR essentially treated all cases individually, without linking them. For this reason, even when these rulings are arranged chronologically, one cannot really speak of the evolution of Strasbourg jurisprudence in this regard.

A lack of citations must be interpreted as an expression of the will of the Court, not a simple omission. Even in *Nagy v. Hungary*, in which, domestically, the Hungarian government correctly cited *X v. Denmark* and *Ahtinen* to support its approach, the ECtHR did not do so.

Since such citations usually give important indications of the reasoning of the ECtHR,[21] it is noteworthy that in this area such references are generally missing.

Furthermore, in most of the cases the Court adjudicated in the form of a decision on the inadmissibility of the application. However, in *Pellegrini*, *Helle* and *Ahtinen*, the Court actually ruled on the merits.

Again, only the complaints of Orthodox priest Skordas and of Mrs. Eskinazi were non-financial in nature—in the other ten cases, financial and property matters, rather than for example theological issues were the main motivations for the complaints.

Lastly, most of the judgments are short or even very short—only a few are of any length, including the most recent, *Nagy*, with its significant number of dissenting opinions.[22]

---

21 For citations in the judgments of various courts on religious matters see F. Cranmer, 'How relevant to the United Kingdom are the "religious" cases of the US Supreme Court', 18 *Ecclesiastical Law Journal* (2016), 300.

22 In the case there are four separate opinions: (a) the dissenting opinion of Judge Sicilianos; (b) the joint dissenting opinion of Judges Sajó, López Guerra, Tsotsoria et Laffranque; (c) the dissenting opinion of Judge Pinto de Albuquerque; and (d) the dissenting opinion of Judge Pejchal. These 4 separate opinions amount in total to over 40 pages.

2 Religious Courts: Their Structures and Their Legal Standing

2.1 *Religious Courts: Sources of Law and Structures*

As stated already in the introduction, almost all churches and religious communities have their own means of dispute settlement. Over the centuries, most Churches developed quite complex systems of courts.[23] The structures of five of the religious courts are of particular relevance to this study, namely:

- the Catholic Church courts (*Pellegrini* and *Šupa*);
- the consistory court of the Church of England (*Tyler*);
- the instances of the Evangelical Courts in Germany;
- the Orthodox courts (*Skordas*);
- the Jewish courts (to a certain extent relevant for *Kohn* and *Eskinazi*, although both courts involved are atypical, see below).

As the Protestant churches have various structures, the judicial system of the largest of them (*Evangelische Kirche in Deutschland*—EKD) is discussed here. The Scandinavian model of the Protestant courts (or more precisely, of the cathedral chapters) is also mentioned, as it is relevant in the cases of *Helle*, *Launikari* and *Ahtinen*.

To complete the picture, some remarks about Muslim dispute resolution are also made, though none of the cases studied here was at any stage pending before a Muslim court/council.

2.1.1 The Catholic Courts

The structure of the Catholic courts is defined in several ecclesial instruments. Their basic structure is set out in the Code of Canon Law of 1983 (*Codex Iuris Canonici*—hereafter CIC) promulgated by Pope John Paul II, especially in Book VII on processes (*De processibus*). More detailed provisions relating to the higher courts are found in the Apostolic Constitution *Pastor Bonus*,[24] issued by Pope John Paul II in 1988. Finally, detailed norms on the structures and procedures of the highest courts are set in specific instruments issued by the Pope for each court. This seemingly complicated legal structure may be illustrated by concrete examples.

In almost every diocese, there is an ecclesiastical court.[25] The court may perform two roles—as the court of first instance for the faithful in the diocese,

---

23 The Quakers are an exception in this regard.

24 Published in *Acta Apostolicae Sedis*, 1988, p. 841.

25 In case a diocese is too small, a court may be established covering more than one diocese, as stated by the CIC can. 1423 and the *Normae pro tribunalis interdioecesanis vel regionalibus aut interregionalibus*, 28 Dec. 1970. The text of the Normae is available under:

and as the court of second instance for another diocese (usually smaller and erected later). For instance, at Wrocław, in Poland,[26] the court is that of first instance for the faithful locally and it is the court of second instance for cases judged by the courts of the dioceses of Legnica and Świdnica, which are smaller and younger dioceses created in the territory of the bishoprics of Wrocław. In cases judged at first instance in Wrocław, appeals lie to the metropolitan court in Poznań. For way of comparison, in Italy there are 33 diocesan and inter-diocesan tribunals, which is a number smaller than the actual number of Italian dioceses.[27]

The judges can be priests or laypersons, must be of sound reputation, doctors or at least licensed in canon law, as required by Canon 1421, and are appointed by the bishop for 5 years.

At the central level, in Rome, there are three tribunals: Apostolic Penitentiary, Tribunal of the Roman Rota and Supreme Tribunal of the Apostolic Signature. The first has competences concerning the sacraments (and is not mentioned in the cases studied here). The latter two have jurisdiction over marriage and administrative cases—they are located in the same building, the Palazzo della Cancelleria in the heart of Rome (and are discussed in section 4 below).

The Roman Rota has a long history. It was established by Pope Innocent IV and its first constitution was given by Pope John XXII in 1331. The Rota adjudicates usually as a third instance court for cases coming from diocesan and metropolitan courts. It is composed of 22 judges, styled 'auditors'. The functions of the Rota are defined in *Pastor Bonus*,[28] as amended most recently by the *motu proprio Quaerit semper* of the Pope Benedict XVI in August 2011:[29] 'The Roman Rota is a court of higher instance at the Apostolic See, usually at the appellate stage, with the purpose of safeguarding rights within the Church; it fosters unity of jurisprudence and, by virtue of its own decisions, provides assistance to lower tribunals.' This echoes Canon 1444 of CIC, according to which the Rota hears appeals from itself or any other tribunal. The Rota is also the administrative tribunal for the Vatican City, according to the *motu proprio Quo civium* of

https://core.ac.uk/reader/83565964, accessed on 5.12.2018 or, in printed form in: P.V. Pinto, *I processi nel codice di diritto canonico*, Vaticano 1993, p. 553–559.

26 All useful pieces of information, incl. documents, are available on the website of the court: http://www.archidiecezja.wroc.pl/index.php?option=com_content&view=article&id=1&Itemid=4, accessed on 18.12.2018.

27 The complete and updated list with all contact data and addresses available at: https://tribunaleinterdiocesanosiculo.it/tribunali-ecclesiastici-in-italia/, accessed on 14.12.2018.

28 See above, op. cit.

29 The online text includes 7 languages versions: http://w2.vatican.va/content/benedict-xvi/en/motu_proprio/documents/hf_ben-xvi_motu-proprio_20110830_quaerit-semper.html.

21 November 1987. The judgments of the Rota are published in *Decisiones seu sententiae Rotae Romanae*, which are not widely accessible. A selection of the judgments in various languages is available online.[30]

The Pope may also establish a national Rota, which fulfills the same tasks as the Roman Rota, to adjudicate on cases from one country, on the basis that it is closer to the interested parties (mainly couples seeking a declaration of the nullity of their marriage). One example is the national Rota in Spain,[31] located with the Apostolic Nunciature in Madrid.[32] It is composed of 7 judges and hears appeals from cases handled in lower courts in the territory of Spain.

Finally, there is the Supreme Tribunal of the Apostolic Signature (*Supremum Tribunal Signaturae Apostolicae*).[33] This was established, more recently than the Rota, by Pope Pius X in 1909, and fulfils three categories of tasks, as described by Articles 121–125 of *Pastor Bonus*. In brief, it adjudicates on: complaints of nullity and petitions for total reinstatement against sentences of the Roman Rota; cases of recourse against singular administrative acts whether issued by the dicasteries of the Roman Curia or approved by them; and other administrative disputes referred to it by the Roman Pontiff or by dicasteries of the Roman Curia, as well as conflicts of competence between these dicasteries. As a general rule, the judgments of the Supreme Tribunal of the Apostolic Signature are not published.[34] It should be noted that the name 'Supreme Tribunal' is to a certain extent misleading, as it is the Pope—the Roman Pontiff—himself who is the supreme judge in the Catholic Church.[35] According to Canon 1405 of CIC, the Roman Pontiff judges the cases: of those who hold the highest civil office of a state; cardinals; legates of the Apostolic See and, in penal cases, bishops; and other cases which he has called to his own judgment. Whilst the last category, theoretically, sets no legal boundaries and allows Pope to judge any case pending before any Catholic court, the three first categories are very limited as regards *ratione personae*. Needless to say, none of the cases judged by the

30 www.cormacburke.or.ke, accessed on 5.12.2018; however this website has not been updated recently.

31 A.C. Ivarez Cortina, and M.J. Villa Robledo, *Repertorio legislativo y jurisprudencia de derecho ecclesiastico español*, Pamplona 1998, p. 110.

32 http://www.nunciaturapostolica.es/tribunalrota.html, accessed on 5.12.2018.

33 http://w2.vatican.va/content/john-paul-ii/en/apost_constitutions/documents/hf_jp-ii_apc_19880628_pastor-bonus-roman-curia.html#TRIBUNALS.

34 T. Białobrzeski, 'Violatio legis w świetle wyroku Najwyższego Trybunału Sygnatury Apostolskiej, c. Castillo Lara z 22.8.1987', in: *PK* 54, no. 3–4 (2011), p. 305.

35 Can. 1442. The Roman Pontiff is the supreme judge for the entire Catholic world; he renders judicial decisions personally, through the ordinary tribunals of the Apostolic See, or through judges to whom he has delegated authority.

Roman Pontiff was a subject of the procedure before the ECtHR in the cases studied here.

In the cases of *Pellegrini* and *Šupa*, the ECtHR did not refer directly to a judgment of a Catholic court—though the Roman Rota and Apostolic Signature were involved at earlier stages of the proceedings, but not immediately before the complaint was lodged with the ECtHR. Therefore, the ECtHR did not have to carry out any analysis in how far the ecclesiastical process corresponds with the (state) process as regards domestic remedies and which instances need to be involved to make sure the domestic remedies were exhausted before recourse to the ECtHR is possible. In this regard, the ECtHR did not examine which court would constitute the final *forum* for the purposes the requirement to exhaust domestic remedies. However, it is extremely improbable that the ECtHR would consider that a determination by the Rota or Apostolic Signature would not have exhausted remedies within the Catholic Church on the basis that the Pope is the final supreme judge in the Church; and, in any event, the Holy See/Vatican City is not party to the ECHR.

2.1.2 The Protestant Courts

The landscape of Protestant courts is as diverse as the Protestant Churches themselves. What follows focusses on the judicial systems operative in the churches involved in the cases before the ECtHR. Three cases originate from Finland. Within the Evangelical Lutheran Church of Finland, judicial tasks are performed by a cathedral chapter, chaired *ex officio* by a local bishop. That a cathedral chapter has both administrative and judicial functions is typical of the Scandinavian Protestant Churches.[36] This is significantly different from the court system of the largest Protestant Church in Europe, namely, the *Evangelische Kirche in Deutschland* (EKD).

The EKD is a federation of the Lutheran, Reformed (Calvinist) and the United Churches in Germany. It consists of 20 *Landeskirchen*, which corresponds rather more closely to the complicated history of the many German principalities and dukedoms than to the contemporary administrative division of the *Bundesrepublik*.[37] Before 1918, Protestant church courts hardly existed in Germany: unlike Catholic courts, they were created after 1918 and the foundation of the Weimar Republic.[38] Currently, the provisions concerning the courts of the EKD are set out in Articles 32a to 32c of the *Grundordnung*, which is

36 A.M. Ciardi, *On the Formation of Cathedral Chapters and Cathedral Culture* (Lund 2016).

37 In Germany, there are 16 Bundesländer.

38 H. Maurer, 'Grundprobleme der kirchlichen Gerichtsbarkeit', in: *Zeitschrift für evangelisches Kirchenrecht*, vol. 17, Heft 1, p. 48.

a basic constitution of the Church.[39] The composition and structure of the courts is more similar to the contemporary structure of state courts and are defined in a Church instrument on EKD courts (*Kirchengerichtsgesetz*).[40] Also, the instrument provides that when church norms are silent on a matter, the matter is governed by secular norms applicable to the Federal Constitutional Court or to other relevant state laws.[41]

The structural and theological diversity of the EKD is mirrored in the diversity of its courts. Each of the regional *Landeskirchen* has its own courts, and on the central level of the EKD there are three institutions: the Church Court (*das Kirchengericht*); the Church Tribunal (*der Kirchengerichtshof*), which is a court of second instance; and the Constitutional Tribunal of the EKD (*der Verfassungsgerichtshof*). All three are in Hanover.

Each court is chaired by a male or female president (*Präsident* or *Präsidentin*). The courts are divided into chambers. According to the *Kirchengerichtsgesetz*, the president of a court and the presidents of the chambers must have a legal qualification in order to sit as a judge according to German state law (*Befähigung zum Richteramt nach deutschem Richtergesetz*). In the case of the church Constitutional Court, apart from the president, two out of four judges must possess such qualifications. The judges are elected for 6 years, re-election is authorised.

The Church Court deals with the cases about discipline, administration, parish councils, labour law, and data protection. The Church Tribunal is divided into senates (e.g. a separate senate for disciplinary cases of the Lutheran Churches and another one for disciplinary cases of other Churches) and handles cases which were in the first instances decided by the Church Court. The competencies of the church's Constitutional Tribunal correspond to the tasks of the national constitutional court, as defined in Articles 32b to 32c of the *Grundordung*. For example, it is responsible for the interpretation of the *Grundordung* of the EKD and adjudicates in competence disputes between the organs of the EKD and the regional churches. Moreover, on request of the Church Court or the Church Tribunal, it monitors compliance with the church

---

39 *Grundordnung der Evangelischen Kirche in Deutschland* of 13.07.1948, most recently amended by a Church Act of 15 Nov. 2017 (ABl. EKD S. 350).

40 Kirchengerichtsgesetz der Evangelischen Kirche in Deutschland (KiGG EKD) of 6 Nov. 2003, published in the Official Journal of the EKD of 15.12.2003, Heft 12/2003, p. 408, with amendments.

41 "Anzuwendende Vorschriften. Im Übrigen finden, soweit kirchengesetzlich nicht etwas anderes bestimmt ist, die Vorschriften des Bundesverfassungsgerichtsgesetzes in der jeweils geltenden Fassung entsprechende Anwendung."

laws (*Kirchengesetze*) and *Grundordnung*. Constitutional Court decisions have the status of a church act (*Kirchengesetze*).

The judgments of the EKD courts are published in a special annex to the Official Journal of the EKD prepared by the Institute for Church Law in Göttingen.[42] More recent decisions are also available in the online data base;[43] most member churches participate in this digital project.

2.1.3 The Courts of the Church of England

The diocesan consistory court when it appeared in the ECtHR cases of *Williamson* and *Tyler* possessed a disciplinary jurisdiction over clergy (under the Ecclesiastical Jurisdiction Measure 1963). However, it is since been replaced in such cases by a new disciplinary tribunal under the Clergy Discipline Measure 2003.[44] The principal jurisdiction of the consistory court today is its faculty jurisdiction, dealing as we have seen above with matters relating to the church building and the churchyard. Nevertheless, the consistory court (presided over by the diocesan chancellor) remains but one of a whole complex of courts in the Church of England.

Beyond the diocese, at the level of the province, there are two appeal courts: the Court of Arches in the Province of Canterbury and the Chancery Court in the Province of York. These courts are independent and each one is not bound by the decisions of the other. However, there is one, very strong and important link: the office of Dean of Arches (president of the Arches Court) and that of the Auditor (president of the Chancery Court) is held by the same person, appointed by the Monarch on the request of both Archbishops.

An appeal from a provincial court may be addressed where the matter relates to doctrine, ceremony or rituals is to the Court of Ecclesiastical Causes Reserved, and in all other matters, to Her Majesty in Privy Council. The Court of Ecclesiastical Causes Reserved was established under the Ecclesiastical Jurisdiction Measure 1963, which provided the modern architecture of the courts of the Church of England. Two judges must be judges (or must have held high judicial office), and three must be (or must have been) bishops: all are appointed by the Sovereign.[45]

---

42 https://www.kirchenrechtliches-institut.de/institut.html.

43 https://www.wbv.de/fis-kirchenrecht.html, accessed on 14.12.2018.

44 http://www.legislation.gov.uk/ukcm/2003/3/contents, accessed on 18.12.2018.

45 M. Hill, *Ecclesiastical Law* (Oxford, 4th edition, 2018), Chapters 6 and 7.

2.1.4 The Orthodox Courts

As with the Protestant Churches, the Orthodox courts have to mirror the complex reality of the Orthodox Churches themselves. Despite the strong ties between the State and Church—e.g. in Greece—the competencies of the church courts are relatively limited. They may hear criminal cases: but only against clergy, not against lay persons.[46] Also, divorces are handled by the Greek state courts; however, church members may request an ecclesiastical court to dissolve the marriage spiritually. While the legal texts seem to be clear, the ECtHR case studied below, *Skordas* (concerning a priest), demonstrates that the reality is slightly more complicated.

2.1.5 The Jewish Courts

The Jewish courts appearing in the cases discussed in this study are somewhat atypical. In the case of *Kohn*, the forum is the Arbitration and Administration Court of the Central Council of Jews (*Schieds- und Verwaltungsgericht des Zentralrates der Juden*) in Germany. In the case of *Eskinazi*, the body is a rabbinical court at Tel Aviv, in Israel.

The *Schieds- und Verwaltungsgericht* in Germany decides a variety of administrative issues concerning the Council and its members. It was founded in 1996. The Higher Court (*das Obere Schieds- und Verwaltungsgericht*) adjudicates in disputes as to the competences of church bodies and in urgent trials. It was established in 2009.[47]

While the *Schieds- und Verwaltungsgericht* is the (second) most recently-established of all the religious courts appearing in the cases discussed in this study, the Jewish religious judicial system has the longest traceable history. The first reference to judges can be found in the book of Deuteronomy, which is traditionally attributed to Moses and so some academics date it to the year 1400 BC. Historically, there were three levels of Jewish courts:

- The Great Sanhendrin, composed of 71 judges, deciding on the most important cases, electing the king, and appointing the judges of smaller sanhedrins;
- Lesser sanhedrins, composed of 23 judges;
- Courts to adjudicate in ordinary and petty cases, each called a Beth Din.[48]

---

46 Ch. Papasthatis, 'Church and State in Greece', in: G. Robbers (ed.), op. cit., p. 115.

47 https://www.zentralratderjuden.de/der-zentralrat/institutionen/schiedsgericht, accessed on 7.12.2018.

48 L. Panafit, 'Juridiction religieuse: Judaïsme', in: F. Messner (ed.), *Dictionnaire Droit des Religions*, Paris 2010, p. 430.

Currently, there are few Batei Din in Europe, e.g. the Beth Din in London, a European Beth Din in Basel, and a Beth Din (Beit-Din) of the German Conference of Orthodox Rabbis.

The Beth Din in London is probably the best known and the most active. Its activities encompass all aspects of contemporary Jewish life, including *Dinei Torah* (court cases), *Gittin* (divorces), *Geirut* (conversions), *Shechita* (Jewish slaughter), *Kashrut*, personal status, and all the trials and tribulations of major communal life. The Beth Din is open to Jews and non-Jews, should both parties agree. Some practical aspects of its work, in particular marriage and divorce, were documented in a research project 'Social Cohesion and Civil Law: Marriage, Divorce and Religious Courts', enriched with the quotations of judges (*dayanim*) and anonymous users, who agreed to participate in the research project.[49] Formally, there is no legal possibility to challenge a decision of the Beth Din by way of appeal to another court. However, nothing prevents the parties from asking the same Beth Din or even another Beth Din, to hear the same case again.[50]

The European Beth Din was established in Basel, Switzerland, and is composed of judges (*dayanim*) from a number of countries[51]—some serve or have served in the London Beth Din. The European Beth Din helps Jewish communities from Germany, Poland, Bulgaria, Czech Republic, Slovakia, Austria, Hungary, Romania, Turkey, Norway, Sweden, Denmark and Finland. It deals with questions relating to the Jewish religious divorces, mediation, questions of conversion, and the settlement of social disputes.

The German Beit Din is attached to the German Conference of Orthodox Rabbis (*Orthodoxe Rabbinerkonferenz*).[52] It is composed of three judges: two appointed by the Israeli Rabbies Conference and one by the Conference of German Rabbis. This ensures that its judgments are respected in Israel. The judges meet around 4 times a year for 3–4-day sessions. This Beit Din was established in 2004, later than the *Schieds- und Verwaltungsgericht* and only after the case of *Kohn* (see below) was decided by the ECtHR.

49 R. Sandberg, G. Douglas, N. Doe, S. Gilliat-Ray, and A. Khan. 'Britain's Religious Tribunals: 'Joint Governance' in Practice', in: *Journal of Legal Studies*, vol. 33, no. 2 (2013), pp. 263–291, doi: 10.1093/ojls/gqs031.

50 G. Douglas [and others]. *Social cohesion and civil law: marriage, divorce and religious courts*, Cardiff 2011, p. 34.

51 However, the website of the Beth Din indicated an address in London and the UK mobile phone for contacts: http://www.europeanbethdin.com/contact.htm, accessed on 7.12.2018.

52 http://www.ordonline.de/der-beit-din-aufgabe-und-funktion, accessed on 7.12.2018.

2.1.6 The Muslim Dispute-Settlement Bodies

To-date, our knowledge of Muslim courts remains limited. Among European countries, where major European Muslim communities are based—the UK, France and Germany—UK researchers seem to have carried out the most extensive studies of Muslim judicial systems. France, due to its *laïcité*, is not particularly interested in the functioning of religious courts, whatever the religious community may be. In Germany, the most significant number of Muslims are Turks and their descendants. This is indeed an important factor, as the role of religious courts in Turkey was significantly reduced or even minimalised by Mustafa Kemal Atatürk while laying the foundations of his newly reformed Turkish State in the 1920s. For these reasons, the UK with its diversified Muslim communities clearly provides a fertile field for research.[53] Last but not least, the remarks of Dr. Rowan Williams, former Archbishop of Canterbury, concerning the potential applicability of *shariah* in the UK in his lecture of 7 February 2008,[54] gave rise to much discussion and subsequent research.

The Muslim communities in the UK have at their disposal both *shariah* councils and an institution, which claims to have a slightly different character, the Muslim Arbitration Tribunal. The best known *shariah* council is the Shariah Council of Birmingham Central Mosque, with its members (judges) participating in various academic conferences in Britain. Two other important councils, which have also been the subject of study, are the Islamic Sharia Council in Leyton, East London and the Muslim Law (Shariah) Council in Ealing, South London.[55] The functioning of the councils is based on the centuries-long traditions[56] of the Islamic courts.[57]

The Muslim Arbitration Tribunal (MAT) operates on the basis of the Sacred Islamic Scriptures and on its own rules of procedure, which are available

53 R. Sandberg, G. Douglas, N. Doe, S. Gilliat-Ray, and A. Khan, 'Britain's Religious Tribunals: 'Joint Governance' in Practice', in: *Journal of Legal Studies*, vol. 33, no. 2 (2013), pp. 263–291, doi: 10.1093/ojls/gqs031, summarises the research project 'Social Cohesion and Civil Law: Marriage, Divorce and Religious Courts'.

54 R. Williams, 'Civil and Religious Law in England—a Religious Perspective', 10 *Ecclesiastical Law Journal* (2008), 262. Presented as part of the Temple Festival 2008 under the auspices of the Temple Church and the Centre of Islamic and Middle East Law at the School of Oriental and African Studies, London.

55 R.M. Cusairi, M. Zahraa, 'Procedure of Issuing Religious Divorce and Resolving Matrimonial Disputes at Shari'ah Councils in the UK', in: *Arab Law Quarterly*, vol. 32, issue 1 (2018).

56 M. Rohe, *Das islamische Recht. Geschichte und Gegenwart*, C.H. Beck, München 2009, p. 34 and f.

57 M.H. Kamali, *Shariah Law, Question and Answers*, Oneworld, London 2017.

publicly online.[58] The judging team must be composed of at least one Islamic scholar and at least one barrister/solicitor practising in England or Wales. The MAT handles a number of everyday life issues, including divorces and forced marriages. As noted by M. Zee, it handles mainly property and commercial issues.[59] All proceedings are carried out in English only, and documents submitted must be in English or with an accompanying translation. According to rule 23 of the MAT: 'No appeal shall be made against any decisions of the Tribunal. This rule shall not prevent any party applying for Judicial Review with permission of the High Court.' Tribunal awards may have civil legal effect under the Arbitration Act of 1996[60]—and any party may approach the (state) court to challenge a decision of the tribunal. Therefore, it is theoretically possible, that a case originating at the MAT would be at a later stage judged by the English (state) courts and could finally be brought to the ECtHR. Such a possibility cannot be excluded—but no such case has reached the Strasbourg yet.

2.2 *Religious Courts and Their Legal Standing in European Countries*

For a case handled by a religious court to reach the European Court of Human Rights, de facto an important condition must be met: a case must originate from a country where the state at least takes note of the existence of the religious court in question. This is not the case everywhere in Europe. In general, as regards the legal standing of religious courts, European countries can be classified in five groups:

- countries where religious courts are (directly or indirectly) part of the state system;
- countries where the decisions of (certain) religious courts are recognised by the state;
- countries where the State and Church are separate and therefore the state courts hesitate to influence the way the religious court work; however such situations may occur;
- countries which take note of the existence of the religious court, but not its jurisprudence; and:
- countries which ignore the presence of religious courts on their territory, and so ignore also their jurisprudence.

---

58 http://matribunal.com/rules.php, accessed on 12.12.2008.

59 M. Zee in her law blog, https://leidenlawblog.nl/index.php/articles/what-happens-at-sharia-councils-part-three-the-muslim-arbitration-tribunal, accessed on 13.12.2018.

60 The text of the act available under https://www.legislation.gov.uk/ukpga/1996/23/pdfs/ukpga_19960023_en.pdf, accessed on 12.12.2018.

2.2.1 The First Group: Religious Courts as a Part of the State System

In a number of European countries, it is a state which creates religious courts—or, to be more precise, courts of certain churches, which are linked to a state. This is a case mainly in countries where state law establishes the internal organisation of a church, including its courts, as it is in England, Finland and Sweden. An outstanding case is Cyprus, which provides in its constitution for the exceptional treatment of courts not of one Church (as in England) or two Churches (as in Finland), but of four Churches (see below).

England with its established Church is the most well-known example in this first group: the law of the Church of England is part of English law (recognised by the ECtHR in the *Tyler* case, see below) and its courts are royal courts. The basis of their structure is provided in the Ecclesiastical Jurisdiction Measure 1963, an instrument approved by Parliament and assented to by the Monarch, as required by the Church of England Assembly (Powers) Act 1919. England also provides perhaps the best example of the interaction between the state courts and the ecclesiastical courts. A state court may order a court of the Church of England to handle the case, prohibit it from doing so, or quash a decision of the church court.

The history of these relations is very rich and longstanding—and there are many collections of the judgments of state and ecclesiastical courts going back to the 16th century. In this context, it may seem surprising that only one English case (*Tyler*, and in slightly different way, *Williamson*) has thus far reached the ECtHR.[61]

The Finnish position is less well-known, but relevant for the ECtHR cases of Helle, Ahtinen, and Launikari. Finnish parliamentary legislation sets out the internal order of the Evangelical-Lutheran Church of Finland, including that for its church courts.[62]

Cyprus is a special case: its Constitution in Article 111 lists four churches, the courts of which are recognised by the state: Orthodox, Maronite, Latin (i.e. Roman-Catholic) and Armenian. While a significant number of issues is currently handled by the state courts, some areas remain within the competence of these religious courts. The State guarantees the execution of their judgments (under Article 111.2, with Article 90.5, of the Constitution).

61 The situation in Wales, Scotland and Northern Ireland is fundamentally different than in England.

62 The Finnish law known as *Kirkkolaki* (1054/1993), the Church Act.

2.2.2 The Second Group: The State Recognises (Some) Judgments of Religious Courts

Some European countries have concluded international treaties with the Holy See, concordats, or other agreements—different names are used.[63] Such agreements cover a number of issues, such as the practice of religion, religious education, pastoral care in hospitals, as well as the autonomy, institutional organisation and law of the church, including the operation of its courts. However, only some states actually respect and, under certain conditions, implement the judgments of Catholic courts, mainly in the matrimonial cases. This is the case in Spain and Italy where a church court declaration of the nullity of a marriage may on the request of one of the parties be sent to a state court for recognition. In Italy this procedure is known as *delibazione* and is relevant to the *Pellegrini* case decided by the ECtHR in 2000 (see section 4). The Italian scholar Finocchiaro has underlined the one-sided character of this process—a church court would not be influenced by a divorce pronounced by a state court.[64]

While in Italy and in Spain the situation seems to be to certain extent a heritage of the past, the Portuguese position is more recent. The respective provisions concerning the recognition of the judgments of the Catholic courts by the state courts are contained in the new concordat signed between the Holy See and Portugal in 2004,[65] under Prime Minister Jose Manuel Barroso, later elected as President of the European Commission. As the respective provision (Article 16 of the 2004 concordat) is relatively short and very clear, it is worth quoting:

> 1. The decisions of the competent ecclesiastical authorities regarding the nullity of a marriage and the pontifical dispensation of a marriage ratified but not consummated, subjected to verification by a superior ecclesiastical body, shall have civil consequences at the request of either party, after revision and confirmation within the terms of Portuguese law and by the competent tribunal of the State.
> 2. To this end, the competent tribunal shall verify:
>   a. that the claims are authentic
>   b. that they have gone through the competent tribunal

63 Needless to say, a number of non-European countries have also concluded such agreements with the Holy See.

64 F. Finocchiaro, *Diritto ecclesiastico*, Bologna 2003, p. 330.

65 V. Canas, 'State and Church in Portugal', in: G. Robbers (ed.), *State and Church in the EU*, op. cit., p. 458. Text of the Concordate: http://www.concordatwatch.eu/showtopic.php?org_id=1361&kb_header_id=4131, accessed on 16.05.2019.

c. that the principles evidence and counter-evidence have been equally respected
d. that the results do not contradict the principles of the public international order of the Portuguese State.

Similar provisions can be found in agreements signed by the Holy See with Slovakia.[66]

2.2.3 The Third Group—Where the State and Church Are Separated and Therefore State Courts Hesitate to Influence or to Set Limits on Religious Courts

This group is perhaps the most interesting: a state and a church mutually respect their own independence, but both share points of common interest. Germany is the best example.

According to Articles 136 to 141 of the *Weimarer Reichsverfassung* of 1919, which through Article 140 of the Basic Law of the Federal Republic of Germany (*Grundgesetz*) of 1949 are still in force, there shall be no state church in Germany.[67] The federal structure of Germany—with its 16 Länder (each with a variety of courts, including civil, administrative, and labour), the Federal Constitutional Court, five other supreme federal courts, and two legally quite different Churches (the Protestant EKD and the Catholic Church) complicate the situation. The understanding of church autonomy has changed over the decades and this is mirrored in the jurisprudence of the German courts, particularly the federal courts, which has been criticised as not very coherent. The fundamental question remains: whether the autonomy of church and state is absolute or whether the state has the right to control the activities and jurisprudence of the courts of these churches.[68]

The most problematic cases are the so-called *Statusklagen*, where a member (or ex-member) of the clergy claims financial benefits from the Church. The

66 M. Moravčikova, 'Slovaquie', in: F. Messner (ed.), *Dictionnaire droit des religions*, Paris 2010, p. 673. Article 10 para. 2 of the Basic Concordate of 2000: "2. The decisions of the Catholic Church with regard to the annulment of marriage and the dissolution of the matrimonial bond are communicated by request by one of the parties concerned of the Republic of Slovakia. The Republic of Slovakia will proceed with the case according to its legal system."

67 The most recent official translation by Ch. Tomuschat, D.P. Currie, D.P. Kommers, and R. Kerr, Bundestag, Berlin 2018.

68 M. Baldus, and S. Muckel (eds.), *Entscheidungen in Kirchensachen*, currently up to vol. 65 (judgments issued between 1.1.2015 and 30.6.2015).

question, whether a given person, in terms of status, is or is not a member of the clergy (*Statusklagen*), must be decided by a religious court. Such matters have been entertained by the state courts with regard to remuneration, pension rights or access to housing. The state courts have refused to adjudicate and declared themselves to be incompetent in such matters and so tacitly accept that only a religious court may issue a judgment in this respect.

Given this legal jigsaw-puzzle it may be thought surprising that only two cases from Germany has reached Strasbourg: the Jewish case of *Kohn*, which was first processed by the *Schieds- und Verwaltungsgericht* of the Central Council of Jews in Germany and the (Protestant) case of Pastor *Reuter* (for both see section 4). However, there have been other cases from Germany decided by the ECtHR (*Obst, Baudler, Mueller* for which see section 3) which have involved matters of internal religious norms such as elements of the Protestant *Kirchengesetz* and Catholic diocesan norms. Despite the fact that all applicants were ministers or employees of various Churches, none of them raised the issue of a religious court as of appropriate forum. Domestically, these cases were exclusively determined by state courts.

The situation is similar in Belgium, the Netherlands and Austria. However, it is more difficult to classify the situation in the *Dudová* and *Duda* cases from the Czech Republic and *Šupa* from Slovakia, which all reached the European Court of Human Rights. The summary of the legal domestic procedures, carried out by the ECtHR and included in its decisions, shows the high level of confusion which belaboured the state courts of various levels in these cases. In both, the intervention of the (state) constitutional courts was needed to clarify the issues: the judges of the lower courts seemed over-challenged with the cases pending before their courts.

Until the *Nagy* case (see section 4), Hungary might have been classified as within the fifth group. The principle of separation between State and Church was stipulated both in the old and new constitution (of 2011). The concordat between the Holy See and Hungary does not contain any specific provisions on Catholic courts. However, *Nagy* demonstrates that while the state courts refused to implement judgments of the religious courts, they also refused to handle the case itself. As a result, the courts of the Reformed Church were therefore the only competent bodies.

2.2.4 The Fourth Group: Countries Which Take Note of the Existence of Religious Courts, But Ignore Their Judgments

This fourth group is partly linked to the second group: the agreements with the Holy See or those with other Churches and religious communities guarantee these bodies freedom as to their internal organisation—so (explicitly or implicitly) they recognise the existence of religious courts. However, the jurisprudence of the courts has no legal effect under state law.

This is the position, for example, in Poland. While the existence of a Catholic court can be understood as an expression of religious autonomy, and is therefore protected by Article 5 of the Concordat of 1993,[69] the judgments of Catholic courts have no civil legal effect. As of 1998, following the ratification of the concordat and respective changes in the Family Code, parties in Poland may conclude a religious marriage, which under certain conditions may has effects in civil law. However, to end a marriage, the spouses must address the state court for a divorce and may petition a Catholic court to obtain declaration of the nullity. A couple which would obtain a religious declaration of the nullity of their marriage by a Catholic court can not request a state court to recognise this judgment and declare the divorce. The Polish Supreme Court, in its judgment of 17 November 2000, firmly rejected such a possibility: a judgment of a church court as to nullity of the marriage has not effect on a state court as regards divorce.[70]

2.2.5 The Fifth Group: Countries Which Ignore the Existence of Religious Courts

France and Slovenia are examples, both having a system *laïcite* characterised by the formal separation of state and religion. The French approach is governed principally by the law on separation of 1905 and its norms on the *associations cultuelles*; the French concordat of 15 July 1801 makes no mentions of ecclesiastical jurisdiction. The Slovenian case is less well-known; its separation system is expressed in Article 7 of the Constitution.[71] As such states do not recognise the existence of religious courts, so they do not respect their judgments.

It is possible only for cases concerning religious courts in those countries belonging to groups 1, 2 and 3 to reach the European Court of Human Rights. For those countries which belong to groups 4 and 5, it is difficult to imagine how a case from a religious court could be lodged with a state court, which is *a sine qua non* for a case to be admitted in Strasbourg.

---

69 Dz.U. (O.J.) of Poland 1998, no. 51, item 318.

70 Court case V CKN 1364/00, commented by B. Rakoczy in Panstwo i Prawo, 2002, p. 110.

71 L. Šturm, 'Church and State in Slovenia', in: G. Robbers (ed.), *State and Church in the EU*, Baden-Baden 2005, p. 475.

3 Important Decisions and Judgments of the European Court (and the European Commission) of Human Rights, Not Referring Directly to Religious Courts

3.1 Karlsson (*1988*)—*The Swedish Government and Appeals from a Diocesan Chapter*

The case of *Karlsson v. Sweden*[72] involved a diocesan chapter of the diocese of Lund which was then part of the Swedish State Church (prior to its disestablishment).[73] As such, the appeal against the chapter's decision was addressed directly to the Swedish government. In point of fact, the state courts were not involved at any stage of the proceedings—nor did the issues come to a confrontation between the state courts and the church courts. However, the case is important in so far as it indicates the reasoning of the Commission in the late 1980s.

In 1984, Jan Åke Karlsson, a priest of the Swedish State Church (*Svenska Kyrkan*), in accordance with legislation on the selection of priests (*lagen om prästval*), applied for the position of vicar at Örekened in the diocese of Lund. Because Mr. Karlsson was known for having a negative attitude towards female priests, and knowing that the parish usually had two priests, the diocesan chapter (responsible for the selection procedure) asked him if he would be willing to co-operate with the other priest in his parish if the latter were a woman. Mr. Karlsson refused to answer this question, claiming that it had a hypothetical character. As a result it was decided that he did not have the necessary qualifications to be appointed as a vicar. In 1985, Karlsson appealed against this decision to the Swedish government seeking its annulment. In the following year the government rejected the appeal. The government stressed that Karlsson's views on women priests were not disqualifying as such, but that it could be expected that he would not cooperate with a female priest in such a way that he could fulfil his duties as vicar.

In March 1986, Karlsson applied to the European Commission of Human Rights in Strasbourg, relying on Articles 9 and 10 of the Convention, read separately and in conjunction with Article 14. In addition, he argued that the government's decision, preventing him from being appointed, violated Articles 11, 13 and 18 of the Convention. Finally, Karlsson claimed that the decision was founded on arbitrary and hypothetical reasoning and could not disqualify him,

---

72 Appl. 12356/86, decision of 8.09.1988, not admissible.

73 For the separation of State and Church, based on a law of 1998, see L. Friedner, 'State and Church in Sweden', in: G. Robbers (ed.), *State and Church in the EU*, Baden-Baden 2005, p. 537.

because, as such, it was contrary to Article 6.2 of the Convention requiring fair process.

In response, the Commission concluded that access to public service—here being a vicar in the Swedish State Church—was not a right guaranteed by the Convention. The Commission also underlined that the Convention did not oblige High Contracting Parties to ensure that churches operating in their territory granted religious freedom to their members and servants, as already stated in the earlier case of *X v. Denmark*, 7374/76[74] (see below in 4.2.3).

The Commission underlined that freedom of conscience is ultimately guaranteed by the possibility of leaving the service of the church, and that the Commission regarded this as an ultimate guarantee of Karlsson's right to freedom of thought, conscience and religion. As such, it considered that his argument based on Article 9 was manifestly ill-founded. The Commission also did not agree that there was an infringement of Article 10 of the Convention. With reference to Article 6.2 the Commission found that since the proceedings were not criminal, Article 6.2 (particularly its presumption of innocence) did not apply. Consequently, in its decision of 8 September 1988, the Commission declared that Karlsson's application was inadmissible.

3.2 Williamson (*1995*)—*Challenging a Church Measure before the English (State) Courts*

The Reverend Paul Williamson's case[75] is the most theological of all the cases studied here. The European Commission of Human Rights (First Chamber), although it considered the application inadmissible, *de facto* clarified the merits. Despite the fact that, during the proceedings, Williamson did not address the matter of church courts and the Commission did not deliberate on their nature, the case raises implicitly issues related to religious adjudication.

Paul Williamson, a priest of the Church of England, opposed the Church's legislation allowing the ordination of women as priests—the Priests (Ordination of Women) Measure 1993[76] and Ordination of Women (Financial Provisions) Measure 1993.[77] After unsuccessful proceedings to challenge the legislation before state courts (Court of Appeal), he complained to the European Commission of Human Rights in Strasbourg. Both of these 1993 measures were adopted by the Church on the basis of the Church of England Assembly

74 Appl. 7374/76, *X v. Denmark*, of 8.02.1976, D.R., p. 5.

75 Appl. 27008/95, decision of 17.05.1995, inadmissible.

76 Canon C 4B (Of Women Priests) reads: "A woman may be ordained to the office of priest if she otherwise satisfies the requirements of Canon C4 as to the persons who may be ordained as priests."

77 http://www.legislation.gov.uk/ukcm/1993/3/contents, accessed on 21.3.2018.

(Powers) Act 1919, an Act of Parliament. In the domestic courts, the applicant argued that the new church legislation was unlawful in so far as it was schismatic and inconsistent with the doctrine of the Church. In addition, through creating a fund to compensate clergy wishing to leave the church as a result of the change, these measures financially burdened the Church and its faithful.

His application for leave to seek judicial review was refused by the Court of Appeal (March 1994); the Master of the Rolls 'found that there was no restriction on the scope of matters relating to the Church of England which could form the subject of a measure, and that once a measure had been duly enacted it had the same invulnerability as an Act of Parliament and its validity could not be challenged in the courts'. The other Court of Appeal judges agreed.

The Chancery Division of the High Court agreed (November 1994) with the request of the Archbishops of Canterbury and York, and Church Commissioners (responsible for property and finance) to strike out the applicant's originating summons of 4 February 1994. The judge ruled that the application only had a theological justification but 'was plainly wrong in law'.

Williamson turned to Strasbourg, claiming that the measure of ordaining women was contrary to the domestic constitutional law and Article 9 of the Convention because he: was required to accept women priests in the Church, which is against his conscience and belief; was forced to raise funds to compensate wishing to leave the church; is a member of a Church which has changed its identity, and he had not been consulted nor given his consent; is bound by an oath, the content of which has changed and he is compromised; faces constructive dismissal for not agreeing with the measure; and the rights of parishioners who must accept female priests have been violated, despite the fact that such a move was against their conscience.

In the decision of 17 May 1995, the Commission noted that the applicant remained in his parish and, despite mentioning the possibility of 'constructive dismissal', his position was not in jeopardy. The Commission stressed that the changes related to church structures rather than to the applicant's beliefs, and that 'his freedom of thought, conscience and religion is maintained, whilst he can leave his office' as the Commission stated in the *Karlsson* case (see above). The Commission noted it was true that the ordination of women became possible after Williamson was ordained. However, it must be borne in mind that the English courts had no doubts about the lawfulness of the changes. Moreover, the Commission emphasized that no employee can rule out possible changes in working conditions, even if his employer is an institution like the Church of England.

At its own initiative, the Commission also referred to Article 14 of the Convention: the possibility of ordaining women as priests was undoubtedly an important step towards equality between women and men in the Church's structure. The Commission also stressed that even if ordaining women were an interference in the freedom of religion of Williamson, it was 'prescribed by law' and so justified under Article 9.2. For this reason, the Commission (First Chamber, chaired by C.L. Rozakis) unanimously declared the application inadmissible.[78]

Commenting on this decision, it should be noted that the applicant did not try to appeal to any of the ecclesiastical courts at all and the proceedings were pending before secular courts. Also, the Commission did not merely consider the application inadmissible on procedural grounds, but in fact ruled as to the merits.

Last but not least, the remarks of the Commission on Article 14 and on the equality of women and men in the Church may be read by some as a veiled attempt to interfere in the internal order of the Church. They could be also read as the first statement of this kind that can be invoked in further judgments. To-date, however, Strasbourg has not returned to this idea with regard to churches and religious associations. As will be seen below, the question of gender and hence of the potential discrimination, is also very much present in cases like *Pellegrini* or *Eskinazi* (see section 4). An attempt to interfere in internal ecclesiastical matters by citing Article 14 at the own initiative of the Court seems even more surprising, since the Court itself condemned States interfering in the questions of church autonomy (see below, point 3.4).

As it will be demonstrated below in section 4, in some European countries, in particular in Germany, Williamson almost certainly would have started by lodging a complaint with an ecclesiastical court. The issue of who is a priest and who is not (in this sense, whether women can be ordained as priests) belongs to the core of internal affairs of the Churches and religious communities. Various German cases, cited below, refer to the principle of autonomy of Church and State. The German state courts would clearly define the Williamson's application as relating to "*innerkirchliche Angelegenheit*" (internal church affair) and would refuse to adjudicate. Even in Poland, where legally speaking there is a clear cut between the State and a Church (which in reality may be somehow blurred), the State always lets the churches decide, who is their priest or not. In particular, a state court would take a stance on a piece of internal ecclesiastical legislation (a measure of the Church of England). However, in case of Mr. Williamson, the English (state) courts felt competent to decide and he

78 It may be worth noticing that among the members of the Chamber were outstanding experts like prof. G. Ress and Sir N. Bratza, whose judgments and decisions will be quoted later.

himself did not try to have his case judged by an ecclesiastical court, which would be natural in many other European states.

3.3 *Implicitly, Only Church Courts Are Competent to Adjudicate a Case of Compulsory Retirement—The Case of the Protestant Clergyman in* X v Federal Republic of Germany *(1981)*[79]

Although the Commission (of Human Rights) did not say so explicitly, by means of *a contrario* reasoning, in Germany only church courts are competent to adjudicate in the case of the retirement of transfer of a cleric. The clergyman of the evangelical church of the Rhineland, Mr. X, was compulsorily retired, as the result of the suppression of his post. He appealed to the German administrative courts. However, these courts, pursuant to Article 137 para. 5 of the *Weimarer Reichsverfassung* of 1919, read together with Article 140 of the current German *Grundgesetz* of 1949, declared themselves incompetent to judge the case, on the basis of the principle of the autonomy of churches. The applicant challenged this decision in Strasbourg, arguing that he had been denied access to a court.

The clergyman argued that according to Article 6.1 of the Convention everyone has the right to 'consider his case within a reasonable time by an independent and impartial tribunal established by law in the determination of his rights and obligations of a civil nature or of any criminal charge against him'. The Commission held that the dismissal in question was not a settlement of civil rights and for this reason did not fall within the scope of the Article. This reasoning was also used in the case of a clergyman of the Danish National Church, in *X v. Denmark*, 7374/76 (discussed in section 4 below, one of the rare cases in which the ECtHR referred to its earlier case-law in this area). The Commission agreed that, unlike in Denmark, there is no state church in Germany. However, as X was compulsorily retired by a Protestant church in the Rhineland—a church with legal personality under public law (*Körperschaft des öffentlichen Rechts*)—it meant that his status as a clergyman was similar (or, citing the Commission) analogous to that of civil servants of the State or of other public bodies. Therefore, the Commission considered that the previous case law relating to dismissal from the public service could also apply to this case. Consequently, a case of compulsory retirement, due to the liquidation of the clergyman's post, fell outside of the scope of Article 6.1 of the Convention and hence was declared incompatible *ratione materiae* with the provisions of the Convention. Therefore, the application was declared inadmissible.

79 Appl. 9501/81, decision of 7.12.1981, inadmissible.

Implicitly, the Commission acknowledged that only church courts have the power to judge such a case.

The reason why this case is analysed in section 3, while a quite similar case *X v. Denmark* is discussed in section 4, is because in the Danish case a consistory court of the *Folkekirke* was involved (even if it actually suspended proceedings for the time of the review of this case by Strasbourg). In the German case, on the other hand, clergyman X did not seek any assistance from the religious courts and addressed the matter directly to the state administrative courts. Also, the most recent case, *Nagy v. Hungary*, although quite similar as regards the outcomes, is treated in section 4, as a part of the process involving the priest Nagy took place before the ecclesiastical courts (in his case at two levels).

3.4 *State Interference in the Functioning of Churches and Religious Associations (Autonomy of Churches and Religious Communities)*

The freedom to operate religious courts is based on and deeply rooted in the principle of the church autonomy. In the most basic sense, autonomy allows for the existence of religious courts. In a second sense, it allows (or requires) States to recognize a religious judicial system and to refrain from any intervention in the functioning of churches and religious communities.

This subsection deals with cases in which State authorities intervened in the functioning of churches and religious associations—and in which, at a later stage, led to a judgment or a decision of the ECtHR. Out of the six cases, three are from Bulgaria, one from Greece, one from Moldova and one from Latvia, which seems to indicate that the problem is of a regional character. All these cases are briefly mentioned, but one (*Holy Synod of the Bulgarian Orthodox Church (Metropolitan Inokentiy) v. Bulgaria*, case 412/03 and 35677/04) is discussed in detail. These judgments are important as they show that the State should refrain from any interference in the operation of churches and religious communities. One may conclude that this rule of non-interference should also apply to the judicial system of churches and religious associations. The cases seem also significant because the ECtHR lists them in its various overviews, underlining their importance, and that of the principles of religious autonomy and non-interference.

Serif v. Greece[80] is chronologically the first one. According to international treaties signed before and after World War I, the Greek government has certain obligations and powers as regards the Muslim community. However, in a specific case the authorities exceeded their powers and violated Article 9 of

80 Case 38178/97, judgment 14.12.1999, final of 14.03.2000, translated into various languages.

the Convention by changing the manner of selection of the muftis and approving one of the candidates. The oldest Bulgarian case is *Hasan and Chaush v. Bulgaria*[81] regarding leadership dispute within the Bulgarian Muslim community. The Bulgarian government carried out changes in the position of the Bulgarian chief mufti (a Muslim religious leader). A governmental agency in 1992 declared the election of Mr. Gendzhev in 1988 as Chief Mufti of the Bulgarians Muslims null and void and proclaimed his removal from that position. The election of a new leader (Mr. Hasan) in his place led to a split within the Community. The ECtHR found this governmental intervention in the functioning of a religious community as a violation of Article 9 and Article 13 of the Convention.[82]

The second Bulgarian case, *Supreme Holy Council of the Muslim Community v. Bulgaria*,[83] dates from roughly the same period, and includes persons who played key roles in *Hasan and Chaush*. Democratic developments within the Bulgarian state led to changes within the leadership of the Muslim religious organisation. The ECtHR held unanimously that there had been a violation of Article 9 of the Convention, as the Bulgarian government introduced changes in the leadership and statute of the Muslim religious community. In *Metropolitan Church of Bessarabia and Others v. Moldova* (appl. 45071/99, judgment of 13 December 2001), Moldova refused to recognize and grant legal personality to the Orthodox Metropolitan Church of Bessarabia, because it separated itself from the Metropolitan Church of Moldova which was recognized by the state. The Court ruled that the lack of legal personality prevented its clergy from performing their duties, and it frustrated the church from protecting its property, which violated Article 9. In the Latvian case of *Mirolubovs v. Latvia*,[84] concerning the community of Old Believers, the ECtHR held that the state authorities responsible for the registration of churches and religious communities[85] had exceeded their powers by evicting one religious community from the temple they occupied.

81 Appl. 30985/96, judgment of 26 Oct. 2000.

82 See the extensive commentary on this case in: S. Muckel (ed.), *Der Islam im öffentlichen Recht des sekulären Verfassungstaates*, D&H, Berlin 2007, p. 286. Also in: L. Lehnhof, 'The European Court's Freedom of Association Cases and the Implications for Islam', in: W.C. Durham, R. Torfs, D. Kirkham, and Ch. Scott (eds.), *Islam, Europe and Emerging Legal Issues*, 2012, p. 304.

83 Appl. 39023/97, the judgment of 16 Dec. 2004, final text of 16 March 2005.

84 Appl. 798/05, judgment 15.9.2009, available only in French.

85 Background and the state organisation in this respect presented by R. Balodis, 'State and Church in Latvia', in: G. Robbers (ed.), *State and Church in the EU*, Baden-Baden 2005, p. 253.

One of the most recent judgments was *Holy Synod of the Bulgarian Orthodox Church (Metropolitan Inokentiy) v. Bulgaria.*[86] The Bulgarian Orthodox Church was led for decades by an archbishop appointed during the communist era with the participation of state authorities. After the political changes in Bulgaria, a new archbishop was appointed by the state authorities. The church subsequently divided into two fractions, one supporting the old leader and one supporting the new leader. However, in 2002–2003 a forced merger of the two churches took place under state supervision. The subject matter of the proceedings was, amongst other things, about 'temples' (the word used by the ECtHR itself) built by members of one fraction were taken over by, and included in the assets of the other fraction. After a number of court proceedings, the ECtHR refrained from requiring restitution of the buildings (from one fraction of the Church to another). The Court ruled that the state's forced joining of the churches constituted unjustifiable state intervention and as would restitution. The ECtHR also cited other judgments on church autonomy, quoted in this subsection: *Serif v. Greece, Hasan and Chaush, Supreme Holy Council of the Muslim Community.*

3.5 *Episodic Roles of Religious Courts*

Religious courts may also play only a marginal role in a case. *D v. France* (1983)[87] involved a pious Jewish couple of the Cohen community and the issue by the husband of a 'letter of repudiation' dismissing his wife. Proceedings were brought before the French state courts. Despite the civil divorce declared by a (civil) regional court, the man refused to give his former wife a letter of repudiation (*get*), arguing that he might want to marry his wife again in the future. Such a letter would forever prevent her from marrying, with himself or with any other man, because Jews belonging to the Cohen group cannot marry a divorced woman. The French Court of Appeal in its judgment of 16 January 1981 disagreed with Mr. D and ordered him to pay his ex-wife 25.000 FRF by way of damages. Moreover, the Rabbinical Tribunal of Paris also urged Mr. D to explain his behaviour. The appearance of the Rabbinical Tribunal in this case, recorded in the judgment of the (civil) Court of Appeal of 16 January 1981, is therefore only an episodic one, it is impossible to find out what result this request brought. Due to the French principle of secularity, it can be presumed with great probability that the decision of the Rabbinical Tribunal would have

86 Appl. 412/03 and 35677/04, judgment of 16.09.2010, final of 21.2.2011.

87 *D v. France*, appl. 10180/82, decision of 6.12.1983, manifestly ill-founded.

had no impact on the judgment of the Court of Appeal[88] The European Court of Human Rights itself did not find violation of Article 9 of the Convention, which Mr. D claimed, and considered the application manifestly ill-founded.

The judgment given in *MPG v. Sweden*,[89] application 20981/92, mentions the fact that the applicant's wife was summoned to appear before a religious court in Teheran. However, this fact did not influence the applicants' situation. The case concerned torture and asylum Mr. M.P.G. would allegedly face if he returned to his homeland, Iran, to appear before a religious court. The European Commission for Human Rights stressed that there were no substantial grounds for believing that the applicant would be exposed to a real risk of being subjected to treatment contrary to Article 3, and declared his application inadmissible.

The Paris Beth Din also appeared episodically as a court supervising *kosher* rules in the case of *Cha'are Shalom Ve Tsedek v. France* (2000),[90] decided by the Grand Chamber. The main actor and decision making body was, however, the Israeli Consistory Association in Paris (Association consistoriale israélite de Paris, ACIP), with the Beth Din being its rabbinical court. The case related to the question is who is authorised to declare food kosher (and receive respective payment for this declaration). The ECtHR judgment contains extensive references to the Bible, in particular to the five first books of the Old Testament, citing the rules concerning food. Not surprisingly, the French 'government emphasized that it was not for the French authorities, bound as they were to respect the principle of secularism, to interfere in a controversy over dogma, but observed that it could not be contested that Chief Rabbi of France, whose opinion on the matter was based on the rulings of the Beth Din (rabbinical court), was qualified to say what was or was not compatible with Jewish observance', as stated in point 66 of the judgment, where the ECtHR quotes the submission of the French government.

More recently, in *El Khoury v. Germany* (application of 8824/09 and 42836/12, judgment of 9 July 2015), a person identified as A.K.—a co-suspect and witness in this case—was the subject of a court order not to leave Lebanon. The order had been issued by a religious court in Lebanon and confirmed by the Lebanese Foreign Ministry and the German Embassy in Beirut. Therefore, although being summoned, A.K. could not appear before the Berlin Regional

88 More about this topic in a very exhaustive analysis of the relations between state and religious laws and courts in France by E. Forey, *État et institions religieuses, contribution à l'étude des relations entre ordres juridiques*, Strasbourg 2007.

89 Appl. 20981/92, decision of 8.4.1993.

90 Appl. 27417/95, judgment of 27.6.2000.

Court. Mr. El Khoury, sitting in a German prison in Berlin, was accused of being a drug dealer. As he could not put more questions to Mr. A.K. (prohibited from leaving Lebanon), he raised the issue of a fair trial within the meaning of Article 6 of the ECHR, claiming that the absence of a witness was violating principles of the Article 6. However, the ECtHR stated in the judgment that A.K. testified extensively on many occasions and that his unavailability at certain stages may not lead to declaring the process as not consistent with the Article 6 para. 1. The ECtHR unanimously declared the application admissible, however did not find violation of Article 6 para. 1 and 3 (d).

3.6 *Cases in Which the Applicants and the Domestic (State) Courts Referred to the Internal Law of Churches and Religious Communities But Made No Reference to Their Religious Courts*

While some judgments may be issued within a decade or more, the time span between cases in this section was much shorter. Actually, two of the judgments were issued on the same days: Schüth[91] and Obst in 2010, while case Baudler and case Müller (and also Reuter, see section 4.9) on the same day in 2011.[92]

Mr. Schüth was an organist in the Catholic Church. He was dismissed after his children said in the kindergarten run by a local Church that they would have half-siblings (thus, illegitimate children of Mr. Schüth). Mr. Schüth did not resort to the (Catholic) church judicial system. Instead, he lodged a complaint with the (state) employment court in Essen, and later with the appeal employment court in Düsseldorf and even with the Federal Employment Tribunal. None of these courts shared the view of the applicant: on the contrary, all of them stressed the importance of marriage and considered adultery as a serious moral fault; dismissal of such an employee was not against the principles enshrined in the German Basic Law of 1949. While the religious courts were not addressed, there was a strong religious element of this case. The German courts, and the European Court of Human Rights referred to internal church law: the Ecclesiastical Employment and Pay Regulations of 1971 and the Basic Regulations of the Catholic Church 1993 on ecclesiastical service in the context of ecclesiastical employment relationships.[93] However, the Court in Strasbourg found in his case violation of the Art. 8, arguing that the notion of private life

91 Appl. 1620/03, judgment of 23.09.2010, final text of 23.12.2010; Case Schüth is available on the website of the ECtHR in 9 languages.

92 G. Robbers comments extensively on the cases in his 'Church Autonomy in the European Court of Human Rights—Recent developments in Germany', *Journal of Law and Religion*, vol. 26, no. 1 (2010–2011), pp. 281–320.

93 Kirchliche Arbeits- und Vergütungsverordnung, Grundordnung der Katholischen Kirche für den kirchlichen Dienst im Rahmen kirchlicher Arbeitsverhältnisse.

should be understood broadly. Moreover, the ECtHR noted the obligation of Mr. Schüth to remain loyal towards the Church, but on the other hand stressed how peculiar was Mr. Schüth's education and work: 'In the Court's opinion, the fact that an employee who has been dismissed by a Church has limited opportunities of finding another job is of particular importance. This is especially true where the employer has a predominant position in a given sector of activity and enjoys certain derogations from the ordinary law, as is the case of the two big Churches in certain regions of Germany, […] or where the dismissed employee has specific qualifications that make it difficult, or even impossible, to find a new job outside the Church, as is the case for the applicant.'

Mr. Obst[94] was a member and employee of the Mormon Church (most recently the Director for Europe, in charge of public relations) who was dismissed for adultery. The Church claimed that adultery is a particularly serious offense against the rules of the Church and that Mr. Obst, who grew up as a Mormon, was well aware of the importance of morality within the Church. Three instances of the German labour courts, including the Federal Labour Court, agreed with the Church and found dismissal without notice justified. The ECtHR found the application admissible, analysed it and issued a judgment (as a chamber). However, also the ECtHR did not find any violation of Article 9 of the ECHR.

The relationship between the decisions in Schüth and Obst have been the subject of considerable academic debate. For example, Ian Leigh suggests that, whilst they have similar facts, the different decisions are justified because the Court carefully weighed the impact on both the religious organisation and employee: while this balance was correctly checked in the case of Mr. Obst, it was not checked in case of Mr. Schüth.[95]

Pastor Baudler[96] was dismissed from his Protestant Churches and complained to the German administrative courts, and later appealed to the Federal Constitutional Court. The latter, applying German case-law, ruled that state courts cannot investigate intra-ecclesiastical matters including cases in which a minister is dismissed from service (for *Statusklagen* see above). Both complained to the European Court of Human Rights, which held the cases inadmissible on the basis that there was no violation of a right guaranteed by German law which would justify a trial under Article 6 of the ECHR. The statement of

94 Appl. 425/03, decision 23.09.2010: admissible, no violation of the Article 8 of the ECHR.

95 I. Leigh, 'Balancing Religious Autonomy and Other Human Rights under the European Convention', in: *Oxford Journal of Law and Religion*, vol. 1, no. 1 (2012), p. 125.

96 *Baudler v. Germany*, appl. 38254/04, decision of 6.12.2011, inadmissible.

the ECtHR in the case of Baudler is in this respect clear[97] (judgment available in French and German, but not in English; however, Mr. Baudler himself was an American citizen). *Baudler* could theoretically be analysed in chapter 4: however, his case was handled by the church authorities (as executive powers), referring to the jurisprudence of the ecclesiastical courts (the ECtHR does not specify the respective cases), but the latter were not involved. In *Reuter*, the German government in its court submission, cited the cases *X v. Denmark* (1976) and *Ahtinen v. Finland* (2008) (see below). The Court itself referred to cases *Dudová* and *Duda* (below) and Ahtinen, but did not repeat the case *X v. Denmark* in its judgment. On the other hand, the Churches acting as third parties (local Evangelical Church of Rhineland and the *Evangelische Kirche in Deutschland*) cited in their observations case *Tyler v. UK* (1993), arguing that in Germany a church is not a part of the public authority (despite being a legal person of public law).

Finally, the case of *Müller*.[98] Mr. and Mrs. Müller were officers in the Salvation Army. For disciplinary reasons, concerning the accounting and the conditions of entrusted real-estates, they first were transferred from Germany to Switzerland; as the Salvation Army did not notice any improvement in their behaviour, they were later dismissed from the service. They lodged complaints against this latter decision with the German labour courts, then with the civil

97 La Cour estime cependant nécessaire de déterminer d'abord si l'article 6 de la Convention trouve à s'appliquer en l'espèce et, en particulier, si les juridictions allemandes étaient saisies d'une contestation portant sur un « droit » de caractère civil reconnu au requérant par le droit interne allemand et propre à faire jouer cet article (Dudová et Duda, décision précitée). Elle rappelle que l'article 6 n'assure aux droits de caractère civil aucun contenu matériel déterminé dans l'ordre juridique des Etats contractants et qu'elle ne saurait créer, par voie d'interprétation de cette disposition, un droit matériel n'ayant aucune base légale dans l'Etat concerné. Elle réaffirme que les garanties de cette disposition ne valent que pour les droits que l'on peut dire, au moins de manière défendable, reconnus en droit interne, qu'ils soient ou non protégés de surcroît par la Convention (Roche c. Royaume-Uni [GC], no 32555/96, § 117, CEDH 2005-X, et Cudak c. Lituanie [GC], no 15869/02, § 45, 23 mars 2010).

La Cour rappelle en outre que, pour apprécier s'il existe un « droit » de caractère civil, au sens de l'article 6 de la Convention, il faut prendre pour point de départ les dispositions du droit national pertinent et l'interprétation qu'en font les juridictions internes (Markovic et autres c. Italie [GC], no 1398/03, § 95, CEDH 2006-XIV, Roche précité, § 120, Masson et Van Zon c. Pays-Bas, 28 septembre 1995, § 49, série A no 327-A, et Ahtinen c. Finlande, no 48907/99, § 38, 23 septembre 2008).

En l'espèce, la Cour note d'abord que la mise en disponibilité du requérant a été fondée sur l'article 57 § 2 no 2 de la loi sur les pasteurs de l'Eglise, disposition qui, comme l'a relevé le tribunal administratif, relevait du droit ecclésiastique et ne faisait pas partie du droit de l'Etat.

98 Appl. 12986/04, declared inadmissible, decision of 6.12.2011.

courts.[99] They were unsuccessful in all trials, because the courts considered that it was an internal church matter. The Federal Court of Justice (*Bundesgerichtshof*) in its judgment on 28 March 2003 recognized that state courts can examine internal church matters only in terms of *Wirksamkeit* (effectiveness), such as the prohibition of lawlessness, good manners and public order but not in terms of *Rechtmässigkeit* (legality). The Court stressed that there was no such violation in the case of Mr. and Mrs. Müller. Mr. and Mrs. Müller resorted to the European Court of Human Rights, arguing that they were denied a right to a court, being a violation of Article 6 of the ECHR. The Court disagreed and considered that there were no rights or freedoms of the Convention violated. The application was unanimously declared inadmissible.[100] Finally, in the case of *Dudová and Duda v. Czech Republic*,[101] who were dismissed from their service within the Church,[102] the lower Czech courts ruled on the basis of the internal law of the Hussite Church and declared themselves to be incompetent in this case. This approach was criticized by the Czech Constitutional Tribunal, which pointed out that the state courts declaring themselves to be incompetent, violated the right of every person to have his/her case decided by an independent and impartial tribunal. This potentially very interesting case, which would be of interest to many Central and Eastern European ex-communist states, the judges of which after 1989 were confronted with the issues so far unknown to them (e.g. applying or not applying internal rules of churches, like canon law) was considered by the ECtHR inadmissible due to the non-exhaustion of domestic legal remedies.

4 Relations between Religious Courts and State Courts in Strasbourg Case-Law

It is submitted that the twelve cases considered in this section actually reflect twelve quite distinct approaches to the matter of religious courts. It is difficult

99 While German labour courts are 'civil' courts in the sense that they are state courts, they constitute a separate branch of the German judiciary.

100 The text is available only in French and reads: "la Cour ne relève aucune apparence de violation des droits et libertés garantis par la Convention ou ses Protocoles". In this regard it is interesting to read dissenting opinions to case Nagy v. Hungary, in particular very passionate opinion of the judge Pejchal, judge in respect of the Czech Republic, appl. 56665/09, discussed in point 3.9.

101 Appl. 40224/98, decision 30.1.2001, inadmissible.

102 Following misunderstandings with their co-employees, Mr. Duda and Ms. Dudová left the service apartment and stopped carrying out their religious mission.

to demonstrate that the cases, taken together, present a single and coherent jurisprudence on the part of the ECtHR with regard to religious courts. There is considerable diversity between the decisions in terms of their treatment of religious courts. The lack of similarities results both from different traditions and legal regulations of church-state relations in the European countries involved, as well as from the different organizational structures of the churches and religious associations.

4.1 *No Answer to the Question Whether the Consistory Courts of the Church of Denmark Provide Proper Legal Protection—(Clergyman)* **X v. Denmark (*1976*)**[103]

X, a clergyman of the Danish National Church (*Folkekirke*), was the incumbent of a parish. He introduced the requirement that before baptising a child, the parents of the child had to complete a course consisting of five classes. The parents appealed against this decision to the Ministry of Ecclesiastical Affairs (or Church Ministry, *Kirkeministeriet*),[104] as X invented this rule by himself. The ministry is the official governmental body which supervises the Church. The ministry acknowledged that a clergyman has no right to impose such conditions and that he should either cease the practice or resign from office. Since X refused to end the practice, the ministry set up a consistory court to function in an advisory capacity. The applicant unsuccessfully requested that the proceedings should take place in public before a consistory court with full judicial capacity. He argued that if the court functioned only in an advisory capacity, he would be deprived of a right to a fair trial, on the basis that in reality the decision would be taken by ministry, not by the consistory court. The consistory court itself suspended its proceedings, pending a decision at Strasbourg.

The clergyman argued before the Commission at Strasbourg that the church limited his freedom of thought, conscience and religion, and so violated Article 9 of the Convention. The Commission did not agree: 'the church is not obliged to provide religious freedom to its servants and members, as is the State, as such, for everyone within its jurisdiction.' The principle emerging from this judgment is called by some commentators the 'principle of voluntarism'.[105] The Commission further stated that Article 9.1 ECHR does not grant the clergyman, as an official of the Church, the right to determine the conditions of

103 Appl. 7374/76, decision of 8 March 1976.

104 The ministry still exists, www.km.dk, accessed on 17.3.2018, the minister in charge is also in charge of culture. The website of the Church ministry is available only in Danish, though.

105 M. Kiviorg, 'Collective religious autonomy versus individual rights: a challenge for the ECtHR?', in: *Review of Central and East European Law* 39 (2014), p. 316.

baptism other than those determined by the highest administrative body, i.e. the ministry. Therefore, the applicant's complaint did not fall within the scope of protection laid down by Article 9 of the Convention.

As to X's argument that he was deprived of right to a trial under Article 6 ECHR (in so far as the consistory court was to be merely advisory) the Commission made two points:

'As far as the applicant would like to have issues of faith or religious practice decided by a tribunal, within the meaning of Article 6, para. 1 of the Convention, the Commission is of the opinion that disputes on such issues do not involve the determination of civil rights and obligations of a criminal charge, within the meaning of the said provision. As far as the applicant claims the right not to be dismissed from his function as a civil servant, the Commission refers to its previous case law according to which litigation concerning access to or dismissal from civil service falls outside the scope of Article 6, para. 1, of the Convention (see, for example, No. 3937/69, Collection of Decisions 32, p. 61).'

The Commission underlined the special position of the church as the Danish National Church, *Folkekirke*. Whereas the national church in Sweden has since been disestablished, for the purposes of Denmark, where the church remains the national church, it is likely that the same decision would be reached today. Above all, the decision indicates Strasbourg's respect for the authority of the Danish ministry to process the case by way of an advisory judicial forum.

4.2 *The Consistory Court of the Church of England as an Impartial Court under Article 6 ECHR*—Tyler (*1993*)[106]

Thomas Tyler, was a priest of the Church of England and ministered in a parish in the Diocese of Chichester as incumbent. In April 1989, a parishioner accused him of adultery with another parishioner. The archdeacon was informed. After a conversation with Tyler, the archdeacon considered that the allegation was unfounded. A second accusation was made by another parishioner, but no inquiry was made. In February 1990 the two parishioners lodged a complaint with the bishop. As a result, Tyler was suspended from his duties. After an initial conversation with the bishop, disciplinary proceedings were commenced against him under the Ecclesiastical Jurisdiction Measure 1963 for conduct unbecoming. In September 1990 the matter was referred to the diocesan (or consistory) court.[107] This court found him guilty of five cases of adultery and deprived him of his living. However, the bishop decided not to deprive him of holy orders.

106 Appl. 21283/93, decision of 5.4.1994, declared inadmissible (by a majority).

107 The consistory court no longer exercised this disciplinary jurisdiction: see above.

Tyler appealed against the judgment to the Arches Court of Canterbury. This ordered a retrial, which took place in the summer of 1991. In the judgment of 18 September 1991, Tyler was found guilty in two cases of adultery and deprived of his living. In May 1992, the Arches Court dismissed his renewed appeal. The British press was keenly interested in the case, and one of the parishioners in question sold her history to one newspaper for £11,500, which intended to publish it immediately after Tyler was found guilty.

Following the dismissal of the appeal by the Arches Court, on 18 November 1992, Tyler filed a complaint with the European Commission of Human Rights. He argued that there had been multiple violations of the Convention, all linked with Article 6 of the Convention: that the Church of England 'was a prosecutor, judge and jury', which violated Article 6.1 ECHR; that the excessive interest of the press impugned his impeccable professional and private past (Tyler referred to Article 6 para. 2, but could have referred also to the Article 8, protection of private life); that there was no fair hearing; that his right to a trial within a reasonable time enshrined in Article 6 para 1. had been violated (3 years, between May 1989 and May 1992); that insufficient evidence had been gathered; and that the case had not been heard by an independent and impartial tribunal.

The government of the United Kingdom replied that the applicant had not exhausted the domestic court remedies, as he could have brought an action to the Arches Court as regards the consistory court. Tyler replied that bringing a case concerning the impartiality to another court (Arches Court), which is appointed in exactly the same way, would not have had too much sense. The European Commission of Human Rights noted that Tyler did not claim the composition of the courts was in contravention of domestic law, however Tyler claimed that this composition could be in violation of the Convention. Therefore, in view of the applicant's inability to invoke the Convention directly in the UK courts, the Commission rejected the Government's submissions as to exhaustion of domestic remedies.

First, the Commission rejected the submission of Tyler that the proceedings to deprive a cleric were criminal in nature. This issue was relevant for Tyler, as in case of criminal offences there are specific provisions (Article 6 para. 2: presumption of innocence) and specific minimum rights (Article 6 para. 3), favourable to the applicant. The Commission noted that the trial in disciplinary cases such as the one at issue, i.e. for 'conduct unbecoming' is not a 'criminal' but a 'conduct' cause; and adultery itself is not a crime in most Member States of the Council of Europe. The UK government in its submission to the Commission also recalled that, according to Commission's own case-law, Article 6 ECHR does not apply to proceedings regarding to the dismissal of civil servants (including the case of *Jakobsson v. Sweden*).[108] The UK government stated also that 'applicants' functions as a priest are more in the nature of public service than they are private professional practice'.

As the Commission could not decide as to the character of the Mr. Tyler's rights, it decided to analyse whether the proceedings were held before an 'independent and impartial tribunal' as required by Article 6 ECHR. First, the Commission stated that 'the law of the Church of England is the same national law as any other branch of law'. The proceedings were based on the Ecclesiastical Jurisdiction Measure 1963 (s. 14(1)), adopted in accordance with the Enabling Act 1919 (see above section 2). The proceedings are initiated only after a confidential conversation between the person concerned and the bishop. Both the complainant and the defendant may be assisted during the trial by advisers and lawyers. As the UK government explained, the consistory court was presided over by the diocesan chancellor who is a qualified and experienced lawyer appointed by the bishop. Commenting on that, the applicant noted that the mere fact of appointing a judge by a bishop means that the court is not independent from the Church of England. In addition, Tyler argued that the UK government did not mention how the diocesan chancellor is assisted by four assessors (two being clergy and two laymen), drawn from a list of people elected by the relevant diocesan synod: this impugns the impartiality of the court, too. The Commission rejected these argument: the arrangements were prescribed by law and the mere fact of that a judge (here the chancellor) is appointed by means of an executive action (here by the bishop) does not mean that the diocesan chancellor and the court are not independent (citing *Sramek v. Austria*).[109] For the Commission, there was a presumption that courts/judges are impartial, and this must be rebutted by evidence to the contrary, e.g. previous political statements of the members of the jury or clear links between the jury and the other party.[110] Tyler himself did not claim that

108 Appl. 10878/84, decision of 4.12.1984. Mr. Jakobsson, a civil engineer with the Swedish National Telecommunication System, was fired after he refused to undergo a medical check-up. The case was declared inadmissible.

109 Appl. 8790/79, judgment of 22.10.1984. The case Sramek related to the issue of the independence of the Austrian local judging body, which was partly appointed by the local executive authority, was housed in the premises of the local authority and its members were remunerated by the local authority, which according to Mr. Sramek meant that they depended on the local authority and hence were not impartial. The ECtHR rejected these claims, stating that these facts are not sufficient to argue the body was not impartial.

110 Le Compte, Van Leuven and De Meyere, judgment of 23.06.1981, Series A no. 43, p. 25, para. 58: appl. 6878/75. The cases referred to medical practitioners, whose suspensions were handled by an organ of a professional organisation (Council of the Ordre des médecins).

the court was biased or that it had been instructed by any external body to decide the case as it did. In conclusion, the Commission considered that both the consistory court and the Arches Court met the requirements regarding independence and impartiality under Article 6 ECHR. As a result, Tyler's application was manifestly ill-founded.

Thirdly, the Commission rejected the claim that the length of the proceedings against Tyler constituted an infringement of Article 6 ECHR. The Commission considered that three years between May 1989 and May 1992 was 'a reasonable time'. Finally, according to the Commission, Tyler was unable to give credence to the fact that the press had an impact on the trial, although it was not to be disputed that one of the protagonists sold her story to the press. As a result, the Commission, by a majority, rejected the application as manifestly ill-founded.

4.3 *The Cathedral Chapter of the Evangelical Lutheran Church of Finland Is Not Impartial:* Helle (*1997*)*; No Comment:* Ahtinen (*2008*)*; as to Length of Process:* Launikari (*2000*)

The Evangelical Lutheran Church of Finland may be classified as a quasi-state church. According to Article 76 of the Constitution of Finland, the Church operates in accordance with the principles set out in a legal instrument prepared by the Synod of the Church, but requiring the approval of the Finnish parliament to be valid, namely 1964 Finnish Church Act (*kyrkkolakki* 635/64). Because of this close relationship between Church and State, appeals against decisions of the cathedral chapters are dealt with by state courts: this happened in *Helle* (1997), *Launikari* (2000) and *Ahtinen* (2008).

4.3.1 The Case of *Helle* (1997)[111]

Mr. Pekka Helle had served since 1952 as a verger in an Evangelical Lutheran parish in Mäntsälä in Finland. As he proudly stated, this function has been performed by his family for four generations. However, he had only been formally appointed as verger by the Parish Council in 1966. His remuneration was set at 75% of the 9th class prescribed for employees of the Finnish Evangelical Lutheran Church. Yet, at the time, it was not determined whether his functions should be classified as full-time, or part-time. It was not until 1988 that Mr. Helle first learned about a decision of the Parish Board of 1977 (in 1966 it was Parish Council, and in 1977 the Parish Board) which classified his function as part-time and, therefore, his pension rights were lower than those who were employed full-time. Mr. Helle complained to the Cathedral Chapter

111 Appl. 20772/92, known also under the number 157/1996/776/977, judgment of 19.12.1997.

(*tuomiokapituli, domkapitlet*) of the Diocese of Helsinki, which, according to the 1964 Finnish Church Act (*kyrkkolakki* 635/64) was 'the court of first instance' for cases concerning complaints about the remuneration of parish officials. As the Cathedral Chapter itself noted in its judgment, 'the cathedral chapter is both an administrative and judicial body of the diocese (section 432 of the 1964 Act). At the relevant time its members included the Bishop, as the chair, three Church assessors and one legal assessor'. The ECtHR also noted that the civil statutory rules on the disqualification of judges extended to the members of the cathedral chapter. Before taking up their duties, the members had to swear a judicial oath (section 436 of the 1964 Act, as noted in point 26 of the ECtHR judgment).

The chapter in a decision of 1 June 1990 admitted that the applicant had the right to appeal against the Parish Board decision of 1977 classifying him as part-time and it accepted that he had not known of this previously. The Chapter held that the Parish Board could not change the terms of employment in 1977, set by the Council in 1966.

In June 1990, the applicant appealed against the decision of the chapter to the Supreme Administrative Court of Finland (SAC), which did not 'find reasons to alter the decision of 1977'. On the other hand, the SAC considered that 'that the cathedral chapter did have jurisdiction to examine the dispute regarding his [Helle's] compensation claim [as regards the difference between his salary and the salary he should be getting as a full-time employee] and therefore referred the case back for fresh examination'. Helle gave the names of six members of the Parish Council who in 1966 were involved in the decision it made at that time. The Chapter met again in August 1991, and decided to uphold the 1966 decision of the Parish Council. The applicant's request, addressed to the Cathedral Chapter to hold an oral hearing, was not mentioned in the Chapter's decision at all. Helle appealed again to the Supreme Administrative Court, which in March 1992 once again upheld the sentence.

In consequence, a complaint was lodged with the European Commission for Human Rights on 28 September 1992. The applicant alleged violation of Article 6.1 ECHR, i.e. the right to be heard in the form of oral proceedings before an independent and impartial tribunal. In addition, he argued that in connection with the refusal to pay the benefits for which he had been working since 1966, his right under Article 1 of the first additional protocol to the Convention was violated, protection of the property. The Commission declared the complaint admissible in violation of Article 6.1, but inadmissible in respect of property matters (Article 1 of the Additional Protocol). In its decision of 15 October 1996, the Commission unanimously decided that the lack of oral proceedings did not constitute an infringement of Article 6.1, and, with

25 to 5 votes, considered that there was no violation of Article 6 as regards the fairness of the proceedings. Mr. Helle then appealed to the European Court of Human Rights, alleging violation of Article 6.1 (due to lack of oral proceedings), and demanded compensation under Article 50.

The Court began by clarifying the relevant substantive and procedural law. Two issues in this respect deserve special attention: the right to be heard in court and the question of the legitimacy of the cathedral chapter. When it joined the European Convention on Human Rights in May 1990, Finland made a reservation that 'the right to be heard [i.e. oral proceedings] cannot be guaranteed in court, as Finnish law does not provide for such a right'. This reservation was withdrawn only in 1996, after the coming into force of a new law in Finland which required courts to provide an oral hearing if so requested by a party; but the law also provided exceptions. At the time at which Helle's case was pending, the law made no provision for an oral hearing.

As to the composition and competence of the cathedral chapter, the ECtHR recalled that according to the Finnish Church Act 1964: everyone has the right to appeal against the decision of a parish council to the cathedral chapter; the chapter consists of the bishop as chair, three church advisers (appointed for three years) and one legal assessor, all of whom take the oath before taking office; and when the chapter considers it necessary to hear or compel the attendance of witnesses, the chapter may ask the secular courts for legal assistance.

The ECtHR recognized that the Supreme Administrative Court was impartial and authorized to hear appeal against a judgment of the cathedral chapter. However, the cathedral chapter, through its position in the Evangelical Lutheran Church, was too closely associated with the employer in this case, i.e. the parish or the diocese. Helle had described the cathedral chapter as an institution which 'lacked the essential qualities for independence and impartiality required of a tribunal' within the meaning of Article 6.1 ECHR (point 38). Nevertheless, the Finnish government argued that decisions of the chapter remained within the sphere of control of the Supreme Administrative Court; therefore, and in accordance with settled ECtHR jurisprudence, no violation of Article 6.1 occurs if the contested decision is subsequently examined by an independent judicial body, one that has full jurisdiction and ensures respect for the guarantees in Article 6.1.[112] *Mutatis mutandis*, this principle and reference to the *Helle* could have been used in the case *Eskinazi* (see below), where the Strasbourg Court noted that the Israeli Supreme Court oversees the jurisprudence of the Israeli rabbinical courts. Even if one would claim certain

112 The jurisprudence included *British-American Tobacco Company v. Netherlands* Appl. 19589/92, judgment of 20.11.1995.

deficiencies as regards rabbinical courts (as Ms. Eskinazi intended to do, but was prevented by her own lawyers), the supervision of the Israeli Supreme Court would rectify any possible defects.

As to the Finnish reservation with regard to an oral hearing, the ECtHR held that this did not constitute a violation of the ECHR. The Court observed, however, some defects in the proceedings, as neither ecclesiastical nor the state bodies did refer to the witness evidence and the minutes of the 1966 meeting, which were key proof in this procedure. Therefore, the ECtHR stated that "the domestic proceedings failed to meet the requirements of Article 6 § 1". These deficiencies were not of fundamental importance: in the conclusions, the ECtHR unanimously declared no violation of Article 6 para. 1 as regards absence of the hearing or fairness of the proceedings.

Last but not least, the ECtHR cited seven of its earlier decisions as inspiring its *Helle* judgment: they are not discussed here, as they are not linked to the issue of religious courts.

4.3.2 *Ahtinen* (2008)[113]

This case involves a 1993 amended version of the Finnish Church Act 1964. Mr. Ahtinen was a pastor in a parish of the Evangelical Lutheran Church of Finland. After receiving warnings from the cathedral chapter (though the reason for these warnings is unknown, and they are not documented in the ECtHR case), he was transferred by the same cathedral chapter to another parish (in another town, 100 km from where he lived). He appealed to the Supreme Administrative Court against the decision of the cathedral chapter. He argued that he was not heard by the chapter. The chapter replied that in the church tradition, as in the army, regarding the transfer of pastors, there is no right to appeal against the decision of the chapter. On 9 March 1999, the Supreme Administrative Court upheld the decision of the cathedral chapter 'without examining the merits of the case' (as stated in point 15 of the ECtHR judgment).

Like Helle, Ahtinen invoked Article 6 ECHR, but the ECtHR decided to treat this matter differently. Because Ahtinen opposed his transfer, the Court first sought to investigate whether being a priest was a civil right within the meaning of Article 6. The Court held—as it did in other cases beginning with *X v. Denmark* 1976—that the rights of a cleric in relation to the Church—his employer—do not constitute a right within the meaning of the Convention. In *Ahtinen*, however, the ECtHR did not cite *X v. Denmark*, nor *X v. Germany* (see above). Consequently, as in previous cases, the ECtHR did not have to decide whether a cathedral chapter meets the requirements of Article 6. Despite the

113 Appl. 48907/99 Ahtinen, judgment of 23.9.2008.

amendment of the Finnish Church Act between the cases of *Helle* and *Ahtinen*, the composition of the cathedral chapter remained the same. Therefore, the Court would presumably have reached the same conclusion as it was in *Helle*.

Like almost all the cases discussed in this paper, *Ahtinen* did not become the subject of debate: it was translated only into Icelandic. However, M. Kiviorg commented on the case in a study on due process norms and religious groups, underlining the principle of church autonomy.[114] P. Slotte too discussed it in her study on ministerial exceptions. However, Slotte did not observe that the Court did not find a violation of the ECHR because it was happy with the situation in Finland, but because being a cleric is not a right protected by Article 6 ECHR.[115]

4.3.3 *Launikari* (2000): Proceedings before a Cathedral Chapter, the National Church Board and the Supreme Administrative Court Violated Article 6 of the Convention

Jaakko Launikari[116] was a minister of the Evangelical Lutheran Church of Finland, head of division in the Centre for Foreign Affairs of the Church. The National Church Board commenced disciplinary proceedings against him. The legal basis for this is unclear—the only thing we know was stated in the decision mentioned in the next sentence. On 19 February 1987, the National Church Board dismissed him from office for having acted in breach of his official duties. The National Church Board, Supreme Administrative Court of Finland and cathedral chapter of the Diocese of Helsinki were involved in the long and complicated process. However, Launikari did not challenge the competence of the two church institutions to adjudicate the matter and the appeal to the Supreme Administrative Court was properly conducted. Therefore, the complaint was lodged with the ECtHR not to discuss issues concerning the competence of the religious and state courts, but with regard to the length of the proceedings, which took more than nine years, ending 12 June 1996. For the purpose of calculating the time, the ECtHR noted that Finland ratified the Convention only on 10 May 1990. Nevertheless, the six years between 1990 and 1996 were deemed to be excessive and the Court (fourth section, chaired by Prof. G. Ress[117]) found unanimously a violation of Article 6, and ordered

114 M. Kiviorg, *Religion and Law in Estonia*, Alphen aan den Rijn 2011, p. 96.

115 P. Slotte, 'The ministerial exception. Theological and legal perspectives from Finland and Europe', in: B.G. Scharffs, A. Maoz, and A. Isaacson Woolley (eds.), *Religious Freedom and the Law: Emerging Contexts for Freedom for and from Religion*, Routledge, Oxford 2018.

116 Appl. 34120/96, judgment of 5 October 2000.

117 Professor Dr. Dr. Dr. h.c. mult. Georg Ress, chair of the Fourth section, was the author's professor at the Europa-Institut at the University of Saarland in Saarbrücken, and encouraged the author to pursue the research in the field of ecclesiastical law.

Finland to pay Launikari for both non-pecuniary damages (for prolongation of the proceedings beyond a reasonable time) and for costs and expenses.

What is surprising about the case is that the ECtHR did not refer to the earlier decision in *X v. Denmark*, in which the Commission held that being the minister of a church is not a civil right within the meaning of the Convention, and therefore the Article 6 does not apply. In *Launikari*, the ECtHR confirmed the admissibility of the case and delivered a judgment.

Another curiosity is this. A few years later, in *Ahtinen*, the ECtHR relied on *X v. Denmark*, as if *Launikari* had not taken place in the meantime. The only difference between *X v. Denmark* and *Ahtinen* on one hand, and *Launikari* on the other, was the fact that both X and Ahtinen were active clergy, exercising pastoral duties, while Launikari, though also a minister, exercised administrative functions in the church's Centre for Foreign Affairs. Did this justify such a significant change in its jurisprudence? The text of the judgment is relatively short and the Court was unanimous, so we have no dissenting or concurring opinions, which could have provided possible answers to this question. However, it seems that the ECtHR was right, avoiding mixing of the pastoral and purely administrative functions of the ministers.

4.4 *Decisions of Church Courts of the Greek Orthodox Church Are Not Subject to Review by State Courts*—Skordas (2000)

Skordas is a very complex case involving proceedings carried out simultaneously in both Orthodox Church courts,[118] and in state civil and criminal courts. This fact significantly hinders the presentation of the case and the timeline of events. Therefore, in order to show what appears to be nervousness and lack of co-ordination on the part of the plaintiff, the dates of the relevant lawsuits and judgments are presented here. This chaotic manner of conducting the case also had negative consequences in the proceedings at Strasbourg.

Evangelos Skordas, a Greek citizen, was a priest of the Orthodox Church. On 7 March 1995, the bishop of the Diocese of Nea Smirni exempted him from his duties as president of the church council of his parish, the reasons for that were not quoted in the ECtHR judgment. In response, Skordas asked to be transferred to the Diocese of Piraeus, the bishop of which wanted to receive him. The Bishop of Nea Smirni refused, however, without giving reasons, and referred the matter to the ecclesiastical court, arguing that Skordas had stopped publishing a journal.[119] In addition, on 11 October 1995, bishop of Nea Smirni ordered the applicant not to celebrate mass for the duration of the disciplinary

118 See section 2 of this paper.

119 Presumable religious journal of the parish; no details on that can be found.

proceedings. On 22 November 1995, the applicant appealed against this decision to the Council of State, which is the Supreme Administrative Court of the Republic of Greece. The diocesan court of Nea Smirni did not issue its judgement until June 1996. In the meantime Skordas had retired by virtue of a decision of the competent State authorities, on 24 January 1996. The Bishop of Nea Smirni continued to refuse permission to transfer him to another diocese where he would be able to provide priestly service without remuneration. In addition, on 6 June 1996, the court of the Diocese of Nea Smirni ordered the Skordas to refrain from all activities as a priest for a period of six months. On 31 July 1996, Mr. Skordas appealed against this order to a civil court in Piraeus (*polimeles protodikio*). Almost a year after Skordas submitted the complaint, on 31 October 1996 the Council of State quashed the decision of the Bishop of Nea Smirni of 11 October of 1995 on the basis that the applicant had not been heard.

Without waiting for the civil court judgment, Skordas filed a lawsuit against the bishop in the first-instance criminal court in Athens (*isangeleas plimmeliodikon*), but the public prosecutor refused to institute proceedings (January 1997), and the refusal was upheld by the appellate court prosecutor (February 1997). Exactly one year after the complaint was filed with the civil court, on 31 July 1997, the civil court in Athens stated that it could not review the bishop's decision to refuse the transfer because it was a 'spiritual' matter.

On 20 October 1998, the court of the Diocese of Nea Smirni held that Skordas had broken its order of 6 June 1996, and, with the consent of the bishops of other dioceses, he had celebrated masses on their territory. The court ordered him to refrain from any priestly ministry for a period of six months. Skordas appealed against this decision to the Council of State—at the time of the proceedings before the Strasbourg Court, this case was still pending. Because Skordas gave interviews to the press, the bishop initiated further disciplinary proceedings, and on 5 July 1999 the church court of the Bishopric of Nea Smirni referred the case to the court of first instance of the Holy Synod (*Protovathmio Sinodiko Dikastirio*). On 18 August 1999, the Bishop of Nea Smirni ordered Skordas not to celebrate mass pending the outcome of the disciplinary process.

Basing on Articles 3, 4 and 9 ECHR, Skordas lodged a complaint with Strasbourg: Article 3 prohibits torture and inhuman treatment or punishment; Article 4 prohibits slavery and forced labour; and Article 9 guarantees freedom of thought, conscience and religion. Interestingly, Skordas did not invoke Article 6 on due process.

The ECtHR—in the Second Section chaired by A.B. Baka—found that the decision of the church court was not subject to judgment by the civil court, as the civil court of Athens had ruled on 31 July 1997. However, the ECtHR stated that the applicant could function as a priest of the Diocese of Nea Smirni, and also, occasionally, in other dioceses. It is a fact that, by virtue of the decision of the church courts, Skordas twice received a ban on celebrating mass and that at present, for the duration of disciplinary proceedings, he was forbidden to perform priestly ministry. However, since the applicant did not challenge the decision of 6 June 1996 and the proceedings before the Council of State regarding the decision of 20 October 1998 were still pending, the ECtHR ruled that Skordas had not exhausted domestic remedies, as required by Article 35.1 of the ECHR, and, on that basis, unanimously dismissed the action as inadmissible.

It is worth noting that while the Council of the State quashed the decision of the Bishop of Nea Smirni (30 October 1996), as it felt competent to judge the case, the civil court in Athens refused to assess the decision of the bishop since it was a spiritual matter (31 July 1997).

Unlike other applicants discussed in this section, Skordas did not invoke Article 6 ECHR. He did not raise at any point the claim that a church (episcopal) court is not sufficiently independent, as was raised in other cases, especially in *Tyler*. While in Tyler the applicant was not successful, in this case Skordas might have tried raising this issue, as the structure of the orthodox courts is different from those of the Church of England. Based on the reading of this case, one may suggest that Skordas had a more personal dispute with the Bishop Nea Smirni than with the whole Church, as it was the case in *Williamson* and *Tyler*. Skordas' own method of proceeding, characterized by haste and lack of coordination, and simultaneous lawsuits in various courts, without waiting for a judgment in each suit, may have contributed to his failure at Strasbourg.

4.5 *Court of Arbitration and Administration of the Central Council of Jews in Germany Entitled to Decide Who Is and Who Is Not a Representative of the Jewish Community*—Kohn (*2000*)

Kohn v. Germany[120] is one of the rare cases mentioned in the academic literature—but this is mainly due to its relevance to the autonomy of churches and religious communities, and not from the point of view of religious courts as such.[121] Elections to a local board (*Vorstand*) of the Jewish community in Hannover led to a split within that community, which triggered a number of other issues with regard to property, in particular concerning the premises (office) of the local board. The arbitration and administrative court of the

120 Application no. 47021/99, the decision is available only in French.

121 Ch. Walter, *Religionsverfassungsrecht in vergleichender und internationaler Perspektive*, Tübingen 2006, p. 385.

Central Council of Jews in Germany (*Schieds- und Verwaltungsgericht beim Zentralrat der Juden in Deutschland*) issued an order (*einstweilige Anordnung*), according to which the newly elected board was authorised to represent the community, and ordered Mr. Kohn, a member of the previous administration council, to leave the premises. The local state court (*Amtsgericht*) indicated that the decision of the Jewish court should not be executed, as it was not issued by a public authority ('n'était pas exécutoire tant qu'elle n'avait pas été enterinée par les pouvoirs public'). The state administrative court in Hannover and the Higher Administrative Court (*Oberwaltungsgericht*) of Lower Saxony were also involved, however they did not respond positively to the request of the applicant. Following this, the Jewish religious community addressed the regional civil court (*Landgericht (LG) in Hannover*). On 2 December 1998 the LG Hannover decided that the case was primarily civil in nature, and ordered Kohn to leave the premises, on the basis of the Civil Code, more precisely on the basis of its Articles 861 and 858. LG Hannover emphasised that because judgments of religious courts are not enforceable, the parties rightly addressed the state courts to enforce the judgment, because solely the state has the monopoly in this regard.[122]

At that same point, a member of the European Parliament, M. Sichrovsky, who belonged to the Austrian liberal party (FPÖ—*Freiheitliche Partei Österreichs*, Freedom Party of Austria), and who was chairman of the association of Jewish unions in Germany (*Bund gesetzestreuer jüdischer Gemeinden in Deutschland*), became interested in the case. Sichrovsky explained that a rabbinical court, Beit Din, on 6 December 1998 revoked the decision of the arbitration and administrative court at the Central Council of Jews.

The German Federal Constitutional Court (*Bundesverfassungsgericht*) issued a decision on this matter on 11 January 1999, dismissing the applicant's request to suspend measures ordered by the regional court. The Constitutional Court confirmed that the civil authorities are not permitted to control the internal decisions of a religious community.

The application was then lodged with the ECtHR, the Fourth Section of which, on 23 March 2000, declared the case inadmissible. The ECtHR, recalling its own jurisprudence, held that the unjustifiable intervention of the State in the internal affairs of a religious community would violate Article 9 ECHR.[123] However, this was not the case here. The Strasbourg Court pointed out, *inter*

---

122 Cependant, le tribunal d'arbitrage ne pouvait lui-même faire exécuter la décision d'expulsion, et c'est pourquoi il devait s'adresser aux tribunaux étatiques, car l'Etat avait le monopole de l'utilisation de la force.

123 For a discussion of these cases, see section 2.4 above.

alia, that Sichrovsky neither annexed a copy of the Beit Din judgment—nor had he furnished information about the composition of the Beit Din. Moreover, Sichrovsky did not identify the Beit Din in question nor did he explain how this Beit Din would be a higher religious court in relation to the arbitration and administrative court of the Central Council of Jews in Germany, which itself is the highest representative body of Jewish communities in Germany. In the absence of this information, the ECtHR agreed that the arbitration and administrative court of the Central Council of Jews in Germany was the appropriate and the highest body to resolve the dispute over the relevant elections within the religious association. The ECtHR agreed with the German Federal Constitutional Court that the state courts had to accept the decisions of the Jewish judicial authorities[124] and provide for their execution.

The decision of the ECtHR seems to be absolutely correct. As regards the relation between the Beth Din and *Schieds- und Verwaltungsgericht beim Zentralrat der Juden*, Mr. Sichrovsky, indeed behaved more like a politician than a lawyer: it is impossible to know from the relevant documentation whether the Beit Din, to which he referred, was the Beth Din in London, the most well-known Beth Din in Europe, or the European Beth Din, established in Basel, Switzerland. If so, the question arises why a Jewish court in London or in Basel should be understood as a higher authority than the arbitration and administrative court of the Central Council of Jews in Germany. If, on the other hand, he was referring to some other Beth Din operating in Germany, he would also have explained which court he actually meant and establish its authority in the matter. It should be recalled that the Beth Din in Germany, appointed by the Conference of Orthodox Rabbis, was established in 2004,[125] which is after the *Kohn* judgment.

---

124 « En effet, comme l'a précisé la Cour constitutionnelle fédérale, les tribunaux allemands ont au contraire souligné qu'il ne leur appartenait pas de s'immiscer dans les affaires internes de la communauté juive de Hanovre, en vertu du principe de l'autonomie des corporations religieuses inscrit dans la Loi fondamentale, et ils ont simplement pris acte de la décision du tribunal d'arbitrage auprès du Consistoire central des juifs en Allemagne désignant les représentants légitimes de cette communauté.

Les tribunaux allemands ont ensuite procédé à l'exécution d'une décision prise par ce tribunal en vertu du droit civil allemand, et là aussi, ils n'avaient pas à vérifier le bien-fondé de cette décision interne à la communauté.

Il s'ensuit que ce grief est manifestement mal fondé au sens de l'article 35 § 3 de la Convention. »

125 http://www.ordonline.de/der-beit-din-aufgabe-und-funktion/ accessed on 28.03.2018.

4.6 *Indirect Criticism of Proceedings before Catholic Courts—* Pellegrini (*2001*)

Pellegrini[126] is arguably the case with the greatest potential impact among all the cases studied here, as it affects the lives of so many Italian Catholics who seek declarations of nullity for their marriages before the church courts. Secondly, it is the only case in which the Rota Romana is involved, and, as we have already seen, neither the Holy See nor the Vatican City State is party to the European Convention on Human Rights.[127] Thirdly, it is one of only a few analysed here which has been translated in other languages: the ECtHR website has links to both Albanian and Spanish translations (which is understandable given the legal standing of Catholic courts in Spain).[128]

Italian citizen Maria Grazia Pellegrini had for years been party to a so-called concordat marriage (*matrimonio concordatario*), a Catholic ecclesiastical marriage having civil law effects. She applied to the district court in Rome for separation, which was granted. A few months later, she received a request from the Ecclesiastical Court of the Lazio Region for her to appear before the court on 1 December 1987 'to answer questions in the matrimonial case Gigliozzi-Pellegrini'. In court, she was informed that her husband A. Gigliozzi, had sought to have the marriage annulled on grounds of consanguinity.

A few days later, the ecclesiastical court, on the basis of the Canon 1688 of the (1983) Code of Canon Law, after summoning both parties and the defender of the (marriage) bond (*defensor vinculis*), ruled that the marriage should be annulled due to consanguinity. The court informed the parties, but failed to send the reasons for its judgment. Pellegrini filed an appeal to the Roman Rota, arguing that she had not received a copy of the judgment, that when she appeared at the Lazio court she did not know about the proceedings and could not properly prepare her defence, and that she did not have the support of a lawyer. The defender of the bond supported her right to appeal, which was agreed by the judge-rapporteur. The meeting of Rota was convened for 13 April 1988, about which the parties were notified on 10 March, at the same time informing that they had 20 days to present their observations. Pellegrini, still without the help of a lawyer, raised the fact that she had neither the time nor the opportunity to properly prepare her case. She also provided information about her

126 Case 30882/96, judgment of 20.7.2001.

127 For a discussion of the judgment, with clearly critical remarks about the Holy See and the Vatican City as regards the human rights, see A. Biggs, *Civil jurisdiction and judgments*, Routledge, Oxford 2015, p. 738.

128 http://hudoc.echr.coe.int/eng?i=001-59604, accessed on 27.2.2018.

financial situation, explaining that her husband's obligation to pay her maintenance were the only source of her income.

The Rota upheld the judgment of the Lazio church court to annul the marriage on the basis of consanguinity, and sent the operative provision of the judgment to the parties. Pellegrini's request to receive the entire judgment, including the reasons for it, was rejected. On 23 November 1988, the Rota declared that the judgment had become final through a decision of a superior ecclesiastical review body, i.e. Rota itself and it was passed to the civil Court of Appeal in Florence for a declaration of enforceability under Italian law (*delibazione*).[129]

According to Article 8.2 of the relevant concordat between the Holy See Italy and Italy, as amended in 1984,[130] the judgment of a church court about the annulment of a marriage, after approval by a higher church court, is enforceable if one of the parties submits an appropriate application to the state court of appeal. This provision is in line with Article 796 et seq. of the Italian Code of Civil Procedure, which provides for a procedure to recognize the judgments of foreign courts. The civil appeal court states whether the decision was issued by a competent court, whether the rights of the parties were respected in accordance with the basic principles of Italian law, and whether other conditions for the recognition of the enforceability of foreign court judgments were met. This procedure was also applied in this case. On 25 September 1989 Pellegrini's 'ex-husband'[131] summoned her to appear before the Court of Appeal in Florence. Pellegrini argued that her rights had been violated in the proceedings and that she had never received the full judgment, nor had she had access to other documents, including observations of the defender of the bond. Consequently, she demanded that the sentence be refused or, alternatively, her former husband be ordered to pay her monthly maintenance for the rest of her life. However, the Court of Appeal rejected her argument and in November 1991 declared the judgment enforceable. The court also ruled that Pellegrini spoke before the church court of the Lazio region and that she had exercised her rights of defence 'irrespective of the special features of proceedings under canon law' and she did not demonstrate her financial needs.

129 This aspect is of central interest in the comments of L.R. Kiestra, *The impact of the ECHR on private international law: An analysis of Strasbourg and selected national case law*, Amsterdam 2013, p. 277–280.

130 S. Berlingo, G. Casuscelli, and A. Pauly (eds.), *Code europeen droit et religions*, Milano 2001, p. 448.

131 The ECtHR uses this term. However, since the marriage was annulled, he was not strictly an ex-husband: 'ex-husband' refers to persons who have divorced, not those whose marriage was annulled.

Dissatisfied with the decision, Pellegrini appealed to the Court of Cassation, arguing, *inter alia*, that the Florence court ignored the following circumstances before the church courts: parties cannot be represented by lawyers; she did not know the reason for the ecclesiastical proceedings until she arrived in court; the defender of the bond was not obliged to submit an appeal; the parties appeal only in person, not through a lawyer; the proceedings were too rapid and she did not have time to prepare; and 'the ecclesiastical court is not particularly autonomous'. Pending the proceedings, Pellegrini again asked the ecclesiastical court for a copy of the documentation filed in the annulment proceedings, but again she had a refusal stating the justification that the operative part of the sentence was sufficient to conduct the proceedings.

The Court of Cassation in 1995 dismissed her case, stressing that the proceedings before the church court were adversarial in character (with implicit statement of the Court that the church proceedings complied with the modern standards and law). As stated by the Court of Cassation, the assistance of a lawyer was not obligatory, but it was not forbidden according to the case-law. Although Pellegrini argued that she had little time to prepare for trial, she did not explain why she would have needed more time. Regarding maintenance, the applicant was not permitted to request financial benefits for the rest of her life and she failed to show that she was entitled to maintenance and that she needed it. After further disputes before state courts, the financial matter was finally settled in 2000 by an agreement between Pellegrini and her former husband.

Pellegrini complained to the European Court of Human Rights. She claimed violation of Article 6.1, arguing: that she was not informed about the possibility of having the assistance of a lawyer; that she had not received the ecclesiastical trial files, which significantly impeded her; that the church court of Lazio heard three witnesses, who allegedly gave evidence in favour of her ex-husband, but she failed to have any access to these statements; and, in the absence of a lawyer, that she felt intimidated by the fact that the ecclesiastical judge was a clergyman. The Italian government replied that the Italian courts acted correctly and lawfully, and Pellegrini herself admitted that she was aware of her relationship of consanguinity with her husband, and as a result, the presence or absence of a lawyer was not important.

As the Holy See and Vatican City are not party to the ECHR, the complaint was brought against the Republic of Italy, the ECtHR judgment itself acknowledges. Thus, the function of the ECtHR was not to determine whether the church courts had observed the standards set out in Article 6 of the Convention, but whether the Italian courts sufficiently verified, before issuing a judgment, that the ecclesiastical process did not violate the principles set out in Article 6.

Pellegrini argued, contrary to the position taken by the Court of Cassation: that in the ecclesiastical proceedings the adversarial principle had not been preserved—that she had not had the opportunity to become acquainted with the testimonies of three witnesses who allegedly testified in favour of her husband; that she could not get access to the position of the defender of the bond; and that she was not accompanied by a lawyer. The civil Court of Appeal and Court of Cassation stressed that Pellegrini had an adversarial process and that the mere fact that the proceedings were pending before so many courts is a guarantee that her rights had been respected. It is worth noting, however, that the lawyer representing Pellegrini officially asked the church courts to have the relevant documents of the ecclesiastical trial sent, but this was refused.

The ECtHR in its judgment of 20 July 2001 found for Pellegrini. The right to a fair trial under Article 6 of the ECtHR includes the opportunity to comment on all the documents that may affect the decision taken in court; this had been well-established in a line of earlier cases.[132]

The ECtHR was critical of the system of 'so-called witnesses' in church proceedings, which clear from the way the ECtHR referred to them, by calling them "so-called witnesses". In terms of the assistance of a lawyer, the ECtHR did not agree with the Italian courts that the applicant might have been aware of the case-law of the ecclesiastical courts in this regard; indeed, the absence of a lawyer to assist her might suggest that Pellegrini was not aware of the relevant case-law.

As a result, the ECtHR unanimously decided that the Italian courts had violated Article 6.1 of the ECHR when they declared that the Rota judgment was enforceable without making sure that the applicant had a fair trial in a process under canon law. The ECtHR awarded her 10 million liras for non-pecuniary losses and ordered Italy to pay the costs of the proceedings.

To avoid such situations in the future, the ECtHR sent its judgment in Italian to the Court of Cassation and the Italian Courts of Appeal; commentaries written by interested lawyers were also published on the legal pages of some important Italian daily newspapers. The Committee of Ministers of the Council

132 *Lobo Machado v Portugal*, appl. 15764/89, judgment of 20.2.1996; *Vermeulen v Belgium*, appl. 19075/91, judgment of 20.2.1996; *Mantovanelli v. France*, appl. 21497/93, judgment of 18.3.1997; *F.R. v Switzerland*, appl. 37292/97, judgment of 28.6.2001.

of Europe considered the case closed after it issued a special resolution, aiming at preventing similar cases in the future.[133]

The ECtHR *Pellegrini* judgment deserves attention for several reasons. Beyond any doubt it, it is critical of the Catholic Church judicial system, specifically the Roman Rota, which due to its history enjoys a special position and prestige within the Church. As mentioned in section 1, the ECtHR could not directly address church courts themselves, primarily for procedural reasons, since the Church as such, the Holy See, or the Vatican City are not party to the ECHR. Secondly, the finding of an obvious violation of human rights by the Catholic courts, including the Roman Rota, even in the first year of the 21st century, required a great deal of courage on the part of the judges of the ECtHR. The loud and widespread criticism of the judgment of the Second Chamber of the ECtHR in *Lautsi*[134] shows that religious symbols (in this case a cross in schoolrooms) are deeply rooted, and attempts to remove them are not easy. The transfer of *Lautsi* to the Grand Chamber of the ECtHR[135] was accompanied by considerable political pressure, including a good number of States involved in the case, and a group of 33 members of the European Parliament. The Grand Chamber, by 15 votes to 2, considered that a cross in a classroom did not violate the rights of parents within the meaning of Article 2 of the Protocol 1 ECHR (right to education) and there was no separate issue under Article 9 of the Convention. Finally, in the context of dual subjectivity in international law, it is worth noting a small detail: in the Pellegrini proceedings and its judgment, the ECtHR refers only to the Vatican, and never to the Holy See.

4.7 *Israeli Rabbinical Courts as Competent Courts*—Eskinazi *and* Chelouche (*2005*)

This section includes a case which is atypical even for the European Court of Human Rights. Readers familiar with ECtHR jurisprudence may rightly claim that many cases are special and unusual, but in one sense *Eskinazi* is extraordinary. The case is commented upon in the literature, but as a case about the Hague Convention and the abduction of children,[136] or else as a 'third-country'

133 Resolution CM/ResDH(2007)126: execution of the judgment of the European Court of Human Rights Pellegrini against Italy; the resolution adopted on 31.10.2007 at the 1007th meeting of the Ministers' Deputies.

134 Appl. 30814/06, judgment of the Chamber of 1.07.2008.

135 Appl. 30814/06, judgment of the Grand Chamber, 18.03.2011, currently (20.05.2019) available on the website of the ECtHR in 21 languages.

136 Family aspects of Eskinazi case: C. Draghici, *The Legitimacy of Family Rights in Strasbourg Case Law: "Living Instrument" or Extinguished Sovereignty*, Oxford and Portland 2017, p. 285.

case, i.e. a case which at least partially refers to a situation taking place outside of the territory of the Parties to the ECHR,[137] in which ECtHR suggests that only in case of 'flagrant denial of justice' would be possible to refuse to recognize a foreign judgment. None of the commentaries raises the issue of the rabbinical courts, which played a role in the case.

Eskinazi, which was declared as inadmissible, is interesting for a number of reasons.[138] The case concerned the parental rights and the place of residence of a girl with three citizenships: Turkish, French and Israeli. This triple citizenship was due to the fact that her mother had French and Turkish citizenships, and the father French and Israeli. The Turkish and Israeli courts were involved, the latter being rabbinical courts. It was the rabbinical courts that caused an additional difficulty in the proceedings, not because of their religious character, but because they were courts in a state which was not a party to the ECHR. For this reason, this case is called *Ethel Teri Eskinazi v. Turkey*, although Israel ordered the return of the daughter to Israel. There are some similarities with *Pellegrini*, in which, similarly, the Holy See was not a party to the ECHR. The ECtHR itself in its decision linked *Eskinazi* to *Pellegrini*.

Eskinazi and Chelouche were a Turkish-Israeli couple, both resident in Israel; both had French citizenship and brought up their daughter together. When the girl was four years old, her mother took her on holiday from Israel to Turkey. During the holiday the mother decided not to return to Israel and applied to the Turkish court (Sarıyer) for divorce; pending this decision of the court, she was granted interim custody of her daughter. Having been informed about this, Chelouche applied to the rabbinical court in Tel-Aviv (*Batei Hadîn Harabaniim Haezori*) to be given full parental custody and at the same time he requested a religious divorce. The rabbinical court ordered the daughter to be returned to Israel within seven days. The order was transmitted through Israeli authorities to the Turkish Ministry of Justice, namely the directorate general of international law and foreign affairs. The Turkish court (Sarıyer) held two hearings and heard both sides (but not the daughter, due to her age). The court decided that the daughter should return to Israel with her father. It is worth emphasizing that the state authorities in Turkey, at the request of the state

137 S. Peers, *EU Justice and Home Affairs Law*, Oxford 2011, p. 622. The third-country aspect also in: O.J. Settem, *Application of the "Fair Hearing" Norm in ECHR Article 6(1) to Civil Proceedings, with Special Emphasis on the Balance Between Procedural Safeguards and Efficiency*, Springer, Heidelberg/New York 2016, p. 137 (Eskinazi case only in a footnote though).

138 Application 14600/05, decision of the Second Section of 5 December 2005, chaired by J.-P. Costa.

authorities of Israel, decided to follow the judgment of the rabbinical court in Tel-Aviv.

Ms. Eskinazi applied to a civil family court in Tel Aviv (*Batei Mispath Lelnyanei Hamishpa'ha*) to challenge the jurisdiction of the rabbinical court, as she was not an Israeli national and she did not reside in Israel, but in Turkey. Interestingly, her Israeli lawyers advised her to withdraw the application, because it 'stood no chance of success'. The case had further complications, based largely on the Convention on the Rights of the Child,[139] and the Convention on the Civil Aspects of International Child Abduction.[140] Ms. Eskinazi claimed that the Turkish courts had for practical purposes ordered the enforcement of a ruling of the Israeli rabbinical court, in which Ms. Eskinazi had not been heard.

The ECtHR analyzed in its judgment the Israeli judicial system (despite the fact that Israel is not a party to the ECHR): 'the Israeli law of 1984, which established the structure of the Israeli legal system, provides—apart from special courts—for three major types of courts: civil, religious and military. The religious courts are governed by the Rabbinical Courts (Marriage and Divorce) Act (Law no. 5713/1953). The laws applicable to Israeli Jews in the sphere of personal status are generally based on the Torah and the Halacha.' The rabbinical court and the grand rabbinical court (Batei Hadîn Harabaniim and Beith Hadîn Harabani Hagadol) are both competent to adjudicate in family matters. They exist in parallel to Israel's state family courts—depending on with which court the complaint is filed first. Over both sets of courts, state and rabbinical, there is a Supreme Court, competent regardless by which route (state or rabbinical) the proceedings take. Thus, the ECtHR confirmed that rabbinical courts are an integral part of the judicial system of Israel and are courts 'established by law'. A parallel may be drawn with *Helle*: the Finnish Supreme Administrative Court oversees cathedral chapters of the Evangelical-Lutheran Church in Finland; the ECtHR did not mention the link.

In her application to the ECtHR, Eskinazi claimed a violation of Article 8 ECHR (right to respect for private and family life); also, that her return to Israel would deprive her of access to courts as provided for by Article 6 ECHR—namely, her case 'would be examined by the rabbinical court to which her husband had applied, that is, a religious court which did not provide the same fundamental guarantees relating to public policy as a secular court, and which she did not in any way recognise as having jurisdiction in the case'. Further,

139 Convention on the Rights of the Child, adopted on 20.11.1989, entered into force 2.09.1990.

140 The Hague Convention on the Civil Aspects of International Child Abduction of 25.10.1980, entered into force on 1 December 1983.

Eskinazi argued that 'The Sarıyer Family Affairs Court had practically adopted the decision of the Rabbinical Court [...], the decision which emanates from a religious court renowned for giving a preference to husbands, but it had also been delivered at the end of summary and not adversarial proceedings'.

Two elements of the ECtHR reasoning are important: 'that even though Israel is not a Contracting Party to the Convention, the rabbinical courts form an integral part of the judicial system in the country, and are "tribunals established by law" within the meaning of Article 6 § 1. As to the religious character of the courts, as mentioned by Ms. Eskinazi, "general argument based on the 'religious nature' of the rabbinical court is not decisive, the Court having never given a ruling to that effect (see, *mutatis mutandis*, *Pellegrini*, cited above, and *Kohn v. Germany*)".

The ECtHR concluded with a thought that seems to be the *leitmotif* of this study: the task of the European Court of Human Rights is not to examine whether one or another court is in principle and in summary consistent with the requirements of the Convention, and in particular with the Article 6. The Court shall only examine whether the proceedings in question before any court or tribunal meet the requirements provided for by Article 6 of the Convention.[141]

4.8 *A Judgment of the Supreme Tribunal of the Apostolic Signature Is in the Slovakian Legal System a Factual Not a Legal Element*—Šupa (2007)[142]

Vladimir Šupa, a Catholic priest, worked for five years in the Pruské parish in Slovakia. In 1994, by a decision of a local bishop, he was to be transferred to another parish (the name does not appear in the file). Šupa did not agree with this decision and filed an objection with the Supreme Court of the Apostolic Signature.[143] The latter decreed the objection inadmissible on 10 February 1996. Šupa was subsequently suspended by his bishop on 2 April 1996. Following this suspension he addressed the Congregation for Clergy at the Vatican, which upheld the decision a few months later (in August 1996).

As the diocesan office stopped paying his remuneration, the applicant requested an order for payment in the district court in Považská Bystrica, which transferred the case to the district court in Nitra. On 17 August 1998, the Nitra court dismissed the claim, finding that according to canon law and civil

141 As internet blogs report, Caroline Chelouche came back to Israel in March 2008—see www.bringseanhome.org, accessed on 12.3.2018.

142 Application no. 72991/01, decision of 6.02.2007.

143 For details, see section 2 of this paper.

legislation of 1991,[144] relations between the applicant and the diocesan office were governed by canon law. The court emphasized that these relations are not labour relations within the meaning of the (Slovakian) Labour Code, hence the latter could not be applied. The district court also referred to the decree of the Supreme Court of the Apostolic Signature of 10 February 1996 and to the fact that the bishop suspended him on 2 April 1996.

The applicant appealed to the regional court in Nitra, arguing that the district court had not examined whether the 'internal rules of the Roman Catholic Church are in accordance with generally binding rules'. Šupa argued that the diocesan office should be treated as his employer because the office paid his health insurance and issued a certificate of employment for social security purposes. The defendant (the diocesan office) pointed out that Šupa had handed over the parish in Pruské to another designated clergyman on 28 August 1994. Since then he had not performed any pastoral duties. In accordance with civil legislation[145] he was not entitled to remuneration.

The regional court in Nitra (10 December 1999) upheld the judgment of the court of first instance: as churches are autonomous, if the state were to define their functions regarding the performance or termination of spiritual services, this would be contrary to the Constitution. Because Šupa had ceased to exercise pastoral duties, and the state court was not in a position to decide whether decisions of the church authorities were justified, the court in Nitra rejected his case. Should the church fail to remunerate someone who is beyond any doubt a priest, the persons concerned may address the ordinary courts.

On 17 July 2000, the applicant filed a complaint with the Slovakian Constitutional Court, alleging violation of the right to judicial protection, equal rights without discrimination, freedom of religion and expression, and decent working conditions, including remuneration.

In its judgment of 31 January 2001, the Constitutional Court found that the complaint should be analysed on the basis of Slovakian law and that the court in Nitra had erred because: 'The ordinary courts considered church law to form a part of the legal and not the factual aspect of the case'. The Court found that the lower courts had issued judgments on the basis of rules that are not a part of the legal order of the Slovakian Republic which does not allow their particular use and so violated the applicant's right under Article 46.1 of the Constitution (right to judicial and other legal protection).

---

144 More precisely, section 5 para. 2 and section 7 para. 1–3 of the Slovakian Act 308/1991.

145 Slovakian Act 219/1949 and Regulations 578/1990 and 187/1997.

Furthermore, the Court found that the diocesan office in Nitra, applying canon law, is not an organ of a public authority, and therefore the civil courts should not have considered its ruling 'as determining a preliminary issue resolved by another authority', as provided in Article 135.2 of the Code of Civil Procedure. While the Slovakian Constitutional Court agreed indirectly that Slovakian courts violated Article 6 of the ECHR, the Constitutional Court lacked power to afford effective redress to the applicant. Therefore, Šupa lodged a complaint with the ECtHR.

In its decision, the ECtHR (Fourth Section, chaired by Sir N. Bratza) noted that, under Article 24.3 of the Constitution of Slovakia, churches and religious associations administer their affairs themselves, including establishing their organs and appointing clergymen independently of state authorities. This is confirmed by Slovakian law (Article 5.2 of Act 308/1991); however, that same law (Article 7.1) provides that persons perform ecclesiastical functions on the basis of authorization from church authorities, acting in accordance with internal regulations and generally binding norms, among them the Slovakian Labour Code. Pursuant to Article 7.3 of this law, churches and religious associations, in accordance with their own regulations, appoint persons to perform spiritual functions or to teach religion and assign them to a prescribed geographical district within which to perform these functions. The amount of salary and other benefits is determined by government Regulation 587/1990 as amended by Regulation 187/1997. This civil regulation once again provides that the period of performing the function, necessary for the calculation of benefits, is determined by a given church. The Ministry of Culture, although it distributes financial resources between individual churches, does not interfere with the internal matters of churches and religious communities.

The Slovakian Code of Civil Procedure provides that courts decide on issues relating to civil law, family law and labour law, unless the law reserves exclusivity in this respect to other authorities. On the other hand, Article 46 of the Slovakian Constitution guarantees everyone the right to legal protection, i.e. a hearing by an independent and impartial tribunal, in accordance with procedure prescribed by law.

The Slovakian Government argued that the domestic judicial remedies were exhausted at the time of the decision issued by the regional court in Nitra on 10 December 1999, and therefore, at the time the appeal was filed with the Strasbourg Court, the period specified in the Article 35 ECHR (6 months after a final decision) has expired. The applicant argued that after the judgment of the Nitra court he resorted to the Slovakian Constitutional Court. However, the ECtHR accepted the government's opinion that, according to applicable law, the Slovak Constitutional Court only issues declaratory judgments and cannot be considered as 'final' within the meaning of Article 35 ECHR, as had been previously determined in cases involving Slovakia.[146] The ECtHR therefore declared the application inadmissible: it was out of time to lodge the case.

4.9 *Reuter: Tacit Confirmation That Courts of the* (*Evangelical Church*) *Are the Only Competent Bodies, in Germany* (*2011*)

The summary of this case may be considered something of an embarrassment for the German judiciary: the applicant lost 5 years to arrive at the exactly same point (i.e. first and second unsuccessful complaint to the German Federal Constitutional Court). The details are as follows.

Pastor Reuter, incumbent in one of the parishes of the Evangelical Church in Rhineland, encountered certain difficulties with his parishioners, represented in the parish board (details unknown). He was first sent for compulsory holidays, then lost his position as incumbent. This led to the significant deterioration of his financial situation. He first addressed the *Verwaltungskammer* (Administrative Chamber) of the Church, which confirmed two times the loss of the incumbent position and corresponding reduction of his income. Pastor Reuter lodged a complaint against these ecclesiastical decisions with the Federal Constitutional Tribunal in Karlsruhe, which rejected the complaint for not having resorted to the respective national courts (6 April 1999).

Basically, at the same time as the main trial, in 1998 Reuter launched another trial concerning his holidays allowance, which he was deprived of. He addressed the *Verwaltungskammer* of the Church, and later the Administrative Court (*Verwaltungsgerichtshof*) of the Evangelical Church, which both denied his rights, as he was no more in active service of the Church.

In December 1999 Mr. Reuter addressed the (State) Administrative Court in Düsseldorf, combining in application both trials mentioned above. He himself noted that the decision concerning his post was an internal decision of the Church, and therefore could not be judged by a state administrative court—however the financial aspect of it, as he claimed, should be handled by a state court. The Administrative Court recalled that the Framework Act on the Public Servants' Law (*Beamtenrechtsrahmengesetz*) provides special provisions for Churches having a status of public law entity and stressed that the Evangelical Church in Rhineland created its own judiciary system. Therefore, the state courts are not competent to adjudicate.

---

146 *Marônek v. Slovakia* and *Stančiak v. Slovakia*, respectively appl. 32686/96, judgment of 19.4.2001, appl. 40345/98, judgment of 12.4.2001.

The Upper Administrative Court (*Oberverwaltungsgericht für das Land Nordrhein-Westfalen*, OVG) confirmed on 3 July 2003 the position of the administrative court. OVG reminded that the Church authority was a public but not a state authority. Moreover, in view of the principle of Church autonomy, the State had to accept the decisions of respective ecclesiastical authorities, regardless of whether or not these decisions respected the fundamental principles of the [German] state legal order.[147]

Mr. Reuter addressed again the Federal Constitutional Court (BVerfG). Although this time he exhausted the domestic remedies, the BVerfG has decided not to accept his application, and did so without giving any reason.[148] This has to be seen as very disappointing: Mr. Reuter's first application was rejected by the BVerfG in April 1999 for not having exhausted domestic remedies; once Mr. Reuter did so—and the state courts did nothing but confirmed the exclusive competence of the ecclesiastical courts—the BVerfG refused in May 2004 even to give reasons why the application was not accepted (obviously, BVerfG could not have played the "domestic remedies" card for the second time).

The European Court of Human Rights did very thorough research and listed in its decision all respective judgments of the German supreme courts: of the Federal Constitutional Court, of the Federal Court of Justice and of the Federal Administrative Court. However, the ECtHR found his application not admissible. This indirectly confirmed the position of the Oberverwaltungsgericht (complete exemption of the ecclesiastical judgments from the state control), despite the judgment of the Federal Tribunal of 28 March 2003,[149] which insisted on the Wirksamkeit (effectiveness) check, i.e. whether an ecclesiastical judgment in question is against the basic principles of the German legal order or against *ordre public*.

The German government took an interesting position: while the government claimed the Article 6 should not be applicable in Mr. Reuter's case, citing (rightly) cases *X v. Denmark*, *X v. Germany*, *Dudová and Duda v the Czech Republic*, *Ahtinen v. Finland*—it alternatively claimed that the ecclesiastical bodies

147 As we read in the ECtHR decision: 'Le droit de la fonction ecclésiastique faisant partie du champ des affaires internes des Eglises, les décisions ecclésiastiques rendues dans ce domaine devaient être respectées par les tribunaux de l'Etat, et ce indépendamment de la question de savoir si les instances ecclésiastiques avaient ou non observé les principes fondamentaux de l'ordre juridique de l'Etat'.

148 As we read in the ECtHR decision, 'Le 10 mai 2004, la Cour constitutionnelle fédérale n'admit pas le recours constitutionnel du requérant (no 2 BvR 1327/03), sans motiver sa décision.'

149 Case V ZR 261/02, also commented in this paper: *Müller v. Germany* (Officers of the Salvation Army).

mentioned in this case conform with the requirements set in Article 6 of the ECHR and that the time of the process was not beyond reasonable deadlines.

4.10 *Courts of the Reformed Church of Hungary Are (by Implication) Competent to Adjudicate and (Explicitly) the State Cannot Assure Enforceability of Ecclesiastical Judgments*—Károly Nagy v. Hungary (*2017*)[150]

Seven years after *Ahtinen*, the issue of religious courts arose once more in the judgment of a Chamber in 2015 and then, 2 years later, in the judgment of the Grand Chamber of the ECtHR in *Nagy v. Hungary*. The decision of the Chamber on 1 December 2015 indicated that the case is not ultimately solved: while the application was declared inadmissible (details of the case below), three of seven judges wrote a joint partly concurring and partly dissenting opinion, while three other judges wrote a joint dissenting opinion. Károly Nagy was a priest in the (Calvinist) Reformed Church of Hungary. Following his statement in a local press he was suspended in June 2005. On 27 September 2005, a first-instance court found that Nagy had committed disciplinary offences and he was removed from service. On 28 March 2006, the church appeal court upheld that decision. Nagy then took the case to the Pest County Labour Court, which stated on 22 December 2006, that according to the Code of Civil Procedure (Article 157(a) in conjunction with Article 130(1)(f)), 'the applicant's claim could not be enforced before domestic courts'. According to the Labour Court, under Statute No. 1 of 2000 on the jurisdiction of the Reformed Church of Hungary (section 2(3)), a pastor's service within the Church was regulated by ecclesiastical law, whereas a lay person's employment with the Church was governed by the State labour law. This decision was upheld on appeal, and the applicant did not apply for review by the Supreme Court.

However, Nagy then lodged a civil action with the Pest Central District Court. The dispute concentrated on various aspects of a clergyman's work and whether similarity with the certain civil law agreements (notably, agency contracts) could justify the intervention of the state courts. The Pest Central District Court dismissed the claim on 2 January 2008, which was confirmed by the Budapest Regional Court on 17 October 2008. Nagy then resorted to the Supreme Court on the basis that he also taught in a school funded by the State.

150 At the time of writing this paper, no academic papers about Nagy case have been published. However, the case Nagy was broadly commented on various websites and portals, dealing with the broad understood freedom of religion: e.g. https://adfinternational.org/news/top-european-court-rules-in-favour-of-church-autonomy/, accessed on 10.09.2018 or http://www.orthodoxru.eu/index.php?content=article&category=news&id=2017-10-23-1&lang=en, accessed on 10.09.2018.

The Supreme Court discontinued the proceedings, stating *inter alia*: 'Under section 15(1) of Act no. IV of 1990 on Freedom of Conscience and Religion and on Churches, the Church is separate from the State. Under sub-section (2), no State coercion can be used to enforce the internal laws and regulations of Churches. [...]. The fact that the agreement entered into under ecclesiastical law resembles a contractual agreement under the Civil Code does not entail State jurisdiction or the enforceability of the claim in a judicial procedure within the meaning of Article 7 of the Civil Code'. Nagy then took the case to Strasbourg.

The judgment of the ECtHR includes several references to the relevant Hungarian law and jurisprudence of the Hungarian Constitutional Court (points 25–33 of the judgment). These references start with the most obvious, i.e. 'The Church and the State shall operate in separation in the Republic of Hungary' (Article 60 of the 1949 Constitution, in force at the time). The extensive quotations from the Hungarian Constitutional Court set the scene: in its decision no. 32/2003, VI.4 AB, it stated: 'where ... a State authority or court established on the basis of State laws lacks competence, the State authority or court must not decide [the matter] by applying ecclesiastical rules, or which church and under what procedure should determine the given dispute; that is, a State authority or court may not interpret or apply ecclesiastical rules'.

The ECtHR also quoted internal laws of the Hungarian Reformed Church, underlining that they do not form part of Hungarian State law. The ECtHR quoted in particular section 34 of the Church Statute 1 of 2000 on the Jurisdiction of the Reformed Church in Hungary on legal disputes concerning the election and appointment of Church officers, etc.

Before giving judgment, the ECtHR (Grand Chamber) recalled that in the Chamber's previous judgment in the same case (1 December 2015) it found no violation of Article 6.1 ECHR on the grounds, that the Supreme Court's decision concerned the interpretation and application of domestic law, which had been neither arbitrary nor manifestly unreasonable.

The Grand Chamber took note of the Government's explanations—that the applicant's claim had not been recognised under State law as an enforceable right, but 'remained in the sphere of natural obligations' and that the 'pecuniary claims based on internal laws and rules of churches were not enforceable by State organs' (point 49 of the judgment).[151] Last but not least, the Government

151 The government remarks may successfully enrich also other discussions: e.g. the statement that "the activities performed by the applicant as pastor did not amount to the provision of services of pecuniary value, that is, those that could be sold on a (secular) market of goods and services."

claimed that State had no obligation under international law to enforce rules of ecclesiastical law.

As the Nagy judgment is quite long and includes many quotations from various acts and judgments of the Hungarian Constitutional Court, it is important not to miss the thought expressed in point 73: 'The fact that the Reformed Church of Hungary had not relied on its exclusive competence in the matter is of no relevance since it is the task of State courts—and not of ecclesiastical authorities—to determine the scope of their jurisdiction' [bold by me, MR].

The ECtHR also came to a conclusion that matters linked to the service of clergy do not constitute a right 'which could be said, at least on arguable grounds, to be recognised under domestic law', so it was not a right within the meaning of Article 6 ECHR. Again, the ECtHR did not refer to previous cases in the field: neither to *X v. Denmark* from 1976, nor to *Ahtinen v. Finland* from 2008. These both cases are not identical with the Nagy case, as Nagy relied much more on the pecuniary value of one of the activities he continued to carry out even after the end of his ecclesiastical service.

Seven judges wrote dissenting opinions.[152] The opinion of Judge Albuquerque deserves special attention—well-structured in 44 paragraphs, it contains references to the previous judgments of the ECtHR, including *Ahtinen, Dudová and Duda, Baudler, Reuter*. Judge Albuquerque also analyzed the legal situation in 39 countries of the Council of Europe, as regards the autonomy of churches and religious communities, as well as the pecuniary claims of employed persons.[153] Judge Pejchal, elected in respect to the Czech Republic, wrote a shorter, but much more passionate dissenting opinion, underlining that Nagy had previously paid state taxes on his church salary. Judge Pejchal continued, asking, for example, 'is it possible that a citizen of a member State of the Council of Europe can find himself outside the jurisdiction of the member State (and thereby outside the jurisdiction of the Convention) as regards

152 Joint Dissenting Opinion of Judges Sajó, López Guerra, Tsotsoria and Laffranque: "In the present case the majority have concluded that the applicant pastor's pecuniary claims, which were indirectly related to his ecclesiastical service, did not constitute a civil right under domestic law. Given the absence of a civil right, the majority asserted that there could be no issue of access to justice. We respectfully dissent. Such an understanding of the case-law not only encourages domestic arbitrariness, but may also deprive many people who enter into ecclesiastical service of the protection of due process. Ultimately, this judgment risks endorsing the position that all appointments and service agreements formed with religious institutions that are subject to internal rules fall outside the jurisdiction of the State. Consequently, such agreements are rendered unreviewable and any rights are unenforceable under domestic law."

153 In the impressive paragraph 20 of the judgment, which includes a number of footnotes to various countries of the Council of Europe.

the litigation pertaining to the sole income received by him and his family, that situation being due only to the fact that the opposite party in the lawsuit is a church? [....] Does this judgment really have its place in contemporary European civilisation?' His dissenting opinion clearly challenges the jurisprudence set by *X v. Denmark* (1976) and *Ahtinen* (2008), or, in other words, calls for a reform and for a new approach in the ECtHR jurisprudence, which would give the ECtHR and the national civil courts more competences in cases so far regarded as internal Church matters. This is still a matter of the national law: however, the jurisprudence of the supreme German courts demonstrate, that two courts (or even two chambers within the same court) may interpret legal provision differently.

5 Conclusions and Outlook

The analysis of the cases studied here shows that the European Court of Human Rights has been confronted in its jurisprudence with the issues concerning the existence of religious courts and with the judgments of these courts. Unlike in the case of a (potential) question addressed by a religious court to the Court of Justice of the Europe Union for preliminary ruling under Article 267 of the Treaty on the functioning of the European Union, which is so far purely theoretical,[154] the issue presented in this paper is real, as proved by twelve cases which have arisen thus far. The cases are indeed very diverse: however, in none of the cases did the ECtHR question the legal nature of a religious court. We can recall that only in one case the Court had doubts about the independence of the religious institution in charge—specifically regarding a cathedral chapter of the Evangelical Lutheran Church in Finland in *Helle*—but then, the supervision of the Finnish Supreme Administrative Court rectified these shortcomings. In the most important case, and probably most well-known, *Pellegrini v. Italy*, the Court resorted to the assessment of the operation of the Italian courts without commenting directly on the actions of Catholic Church courts (including the Roman Rota). In other cases, the Court managed to avoid answering questions about the jurisdiction or the character of religious courts within the meaning of the Article 6 ECHR, whether trials were trials before

154 M. Rynkowski, 'A religious court as a court of a Member State under Article 267 of the TFUE', in: R. Potz, and W. Wieshaider (eds.), *Jurisdictions religieuses et l'État*, Granada 2015, p. 245. However, it should be noted, that after the judgment of the Grand Chamber of the Court of Justice of the EU of 11 Sept. 2018 in case C-68/17 *IR vs JQ*, the moment when a religious court will ask for a preliminary ruling, is not impossible anymore.

an independent and impartial tribunal. The conclusion contained in the decision in *Eskinazi* (although the application itself was considered inadmissible) seems to best reflect the essence of the matter and, at the same time, the ECtHR's view of religious courts in the contemporary European legal order.

The general conclusion would be that when a bishop, synod or other religious authority appoints members of a religious court, such court is independent within the meaning of the European Convention. When a bishop sits on the adjudicating body, as in the case of the diocesan chapter of the Evangelical Lutheran Church of Finland, such a court itself does not meet the requirements of independence, as a bishop, representing the local church, happens to be a party in the pending case. The (Finnish) situation is mitigated by the fact that the Supreme Administrative Court of Finland carries out a control of the jurisprudence of the chapters.

It seems, therefore, that the ECtHR's jurisprudence regarding religious courts is fully in line with the Charles de Montesquieu theory of the separation of powers, as expressed in his famous treaty "*De l'esprit des loix*" from 1748, which is a fundament to many contemporary democratic constitutions. When a bishop, who is the executive authority within the church, sits personally in court, he breaks the rule of the tripartite system/separation of powers. When a bishop appoints judges, as is the case in the Church of England or Catholic, Article 6 seems to be respected. Although the Court (idem for the Commission before) did not refer directly to Montesquieu or to the principle of the separation of powers in the aforementioned cases, this idea seems to have guided the judges of the ECtHR. Finally, one can anecdotally refer to the English case from 1680, *Sheffield v. Canterbury*.[155] According to the precedent in this case, the Archbishop of Canterbury himself can sit in the Arches Court if he so wishes. Thus, the presence of the archbishop in the composition of judges would make this court fail to meet the requirements of the European Convention on Human Rights.

While the jurisprudence of the courts of the Church of England dates back to the 16th century, the various civil courts also have jurisprudence on religion. Recently this question reached yet another time even the Court of Justice of the EU. In the case IR, decided on 11 September 2018, the CJEU had to judge whether dismissal of a director of a Catholic hospital is lawful, since his married civilly for the second time.[156]

155 *Sheffield v Canterbury*, 2 Show 146, 89 ER 849, cited by: *The Digest. Annotated British, Commonwealth and European Cases*, vol. 19(2), London 1997, p. 235.

156 Judgment of 11.09.2018, Grand Chamber of the CJ of the EU, *IR v JQ*.

As demonstrated above, the twelve cases studied here were brought to the ECtHR and were decided mainly in the 1990s and in the first two decades of this century.[157] *Nagy v. Hungary* of 2017, and in particular a number and the content of the dissenting opinions shows, that the issue is not closed and diverging opinions in the years to come can be expected. That makes the issue of the religious courts in the jurisprudence of the ECtHR even more interesting.

Bibliography

Cases Quoted

European Court of Human Rights and European Commission of Human Rights

Ahtinen v. Finland, appl. 48907/99, judgment of 31.5.2005.

British-American Tobacco Company v. The Netherlands, appl. 19589/92, judgment of 20.11.1995.

Cha'are Shalom Ve Tsedek v. France, appl. 27417/95, judgment of 27.6.2000.

D v. France, appl. 10180/82, decision of 6.12.1983, manifestly ill-founded.

Dudová and Duda v. Czech Republic, appl. 40224/98, judgment of 30.1.2001.

Eskinazi and Chelouche v. Turkey, appl. 14600/05, decision of 5.12.2005.

F.R. v Switzerland, appl. 37292/97, judgment of 28.6.2001.

Hasan and Chaush v. Bulgaria, appl. 30985/96, judgment of 26.10.2000.

Helle v. Finland, appl. 20772/92, judgment of 19.12.1997.

Holy Synod of the Bulgarian Orthodox Church (Metropolitan Inokentiy) v. Bulgaria, appl. 412/03 and 35677/04, judgment of 16.9.2010, final of 21.2.2011.

Jakobsson v Sweden, appl. 10878/84, judgment of 4.12.1984.

Karlsson v Sweden, appl. 12356/86, decision of 8.9.1988.

Kohn v. Germany, appl. 47021/99, decision of 23.3.2000.

Lautsi v Italy, appl. 30814/06, Chamber: of 3.11.2009 r., judgment of Grand Chamber of 18.3.2011.

Lobo Machado v Portugal, appl. 15764/89, judgment of 20.2.1996.

Mantovanelli v. France, appl. 21497/93, judgment of 18.3.1997.

Marônek v. Slovakia, appl. 32686/96, judgment of 19.4.2001.

Mirolubovs v Latvia, appl. 798/05, judgment of 15.9.2009.

Nagy v. Hungary, appl. 56665/2009, judgment of 14.09.2017.

157 The dynamics of the developments in the area of religious freedom in the jurisprudence of the ECtHR was also noted and underlined by I. Leigh, 'Balancing Religious Autonomy and Other Human Rights under the European Convention', in: *Oxford Journal of Law and Religion*, vol. 1, no. 1 (2012), p. 125.

Obst v. Germany, appl. 425/03, judgment of 23.9.2010, final 23.12.2010.
Orthodox Metropolitan Church of Bessarabia and Others v. Moldova, appl. 45071/99, judgment of 13.12.2001.
Pellegrini v. Italy, appl. 30882/96, judgment of 20.7.2001.
Reuter v. Germany, appl. 39775/04, decision of 6.12.2011.
Schüth v Germany, appl. 1620/03, judgment of 23.9.2010, final 23.12.2010.
Serif v. Greece, appl. 38178/97, judgment of 14.12.1999 r., final of 14.3.2000.
Skordas v. Greece, appl. 48895/99, decision of 15.6.2000.
Sramek v. Austria, appl. 8790/79, judgment of 22.10.1984.
Šupa v. Slovakia, appl. 72991/01, judgment of 31.01.2001.
Tyler v. UK, appl. 21283/93, decision of 5.4.1994.
Vermeulen v Belgium, appl. 19075/91, judgment of 20.2.1996.
Williamson v. UK, appl. 27008/95, decision of 17.5.1995.
X v. Denmark, appl. 7374/76, decision of 8.03.1976.
X v Germany, appl. 9501/81, decision of 7.12.1981.
The Supreme Holy Council of the Muslim Community v. Bulgaria, appl. 39023/97, judgment of 16.12.2004, final of 16.3.2005.

Literature

Balodis, R., 'State and Church in Latvia', in: G. Robbers (ed.), *State and Church in the EU*, Baden-Baden 2005.
Berlingo, S., Casuscelli, G., and Pauly, A. (eds.), *Code européen droit et religions*, Milano 2001.
Białobrzeski, T., 'Violatio legis w świetle wyroku Najwyższego Trybunału Sygnatury Apostolskiej, c. Castillo Lara z 22.8.1987', in: *Prawo Kanoniczne*, vol. 54, no. 3–4 (2011), p. 305.
Biggs, A., *Civil jurisdiction and judgments*, Routledge, Oxford 2015.
Ciardi, A.M., *On the Formation of Cathedral Chapters and Cathedral Culture*, Lund 2016.
Cranmer, F., 'How relevant to the United Kingdom are the "religious" cases of the US Supreme Court?', in: *Ecclesiastical Law Journal*, vol. 18 (2016).
Cusairi, R.M., and Zahraa, M., 'Procedure of Issuing Religious Divorce and Resolving Matrimonial Disputes at Shari'ah Councils in the UK', in: *Arab Law Quarterly*, vol. 32, issue 1 (2018).
Doe, N., *Christian Law. Contemporary Principles*, Cambridge 2011.
Doe, N., *Law and Religion in Europe, A Comparative Introduction*, Oxford 2011.
Draghici, C., *The Legitimacy of Family Rights in Strasbourg Case Law: "Living Instrument" or Extinguished Sovereignty*, Oxford and Portland 2017, p. 285.
Finochiaro, F., *Diritto ecclesiastico*, Bologna 2003.
Friedner, L., 'State and Church in Sweden', in: G. Robbers (ed.), *State and Church in the EU*, Baden-Baden 2005.

Forey, E., *État et institions religieuses, contribution à l'étude des relations entre ordres juridiques*, Strasbourg 2007.

Kamali, M.H., *Shariah Law, Question and answers*, Oneworld, London 2017.

Kiestra, L.R., *The impact of the ECHR on private international law: An analysis of Strasbourg and selected national case law*, Amsterdam 2013.

Kiviorg, M., 'Collective religious autonomy versus individual rights: a challenge for the ECtHR?', in: *Review of Central and East European Law* 39 (2014).

Kiviorg, M., *Religion and Law in Estonia*, Alphen aan den Rijn 2011, p. 96.

Lehnhof, L., 'The European Court's Freedom of Association Cases and the Implications for Islam', in: W.C. Durham, R. Torfs, D. Kirkham and Ch. Scott (eds.), *Islam, Europe and Emerging Legal Issues*, Farnham 2012.

Leigh, I., 'Balancing Religious Autonomy and Other Human Rights under the European Convention', in: *Oxford Journal of Law and Religion*, vol. 1, no. 1 (2012), p. 109.

Maurer, H., 'Grundprobleme der kirchlichen Gerichtsbarkeit', in: *Zeitschrift für evangelisches Kirchenrecht*, vol. 17, Heft 1, p. 48.

McCrea, R., 'Art. 10 [of the Charter] Freedom of Thought, Conscience and Religion', in: S. Peers, T. Hervey, J. Kenner, and A. Ward (eds.), *The EU Charter of Fundamental Rights*, Oxford and Portland 2014.

McGregor, A., 'Religion, Doctrine and Ecclesiastical Courts', in: *Ecclesiastical Law Journal*, vol. 13 (2011).

Messner, F. (ed.), *Dictionnaire droit des religions*, Paris 2010.

Moravčikova, M., 'Slovaquie', in: F. Messner (ed.), *Dictionnaire droit des religions*, Paris 2010.

Muckel, S. (ed.), *Der Islam im offentlichen Recht des sekularen Verfassungstaates*, D&H, Berlin 2007.

Panafit, L., 'Juridiction religieuse: Judaïsme', in: F. Messner (ed.), *Dictionnaire Droit des Religions*, Paris 2010, p. 430.

Papasthatis, Ch., 'State and Church in Greece', in: G. Robbers (ed.). *State and Church in the EU*, Baden-Baden 2005.

Peers, S., *EU Justice and Home Affairs Law*, Oxford 2011.

Peers, S., Hervey, T., Kenner, J., and Ward, A. (eds.), *The EU Charter of fundamental rights*, Oxford and Portland 2014.

Pinto, P.V., *I processi nel codice di diritto canonico*, Vaticano 1993.

Rengeling, H.-W., and Szczekalla, P. (eds.), *Grundrechte in der Europäischen Union, Charta der Grundrechte und Allgemeine Rechtsgrundsätze*, Köln 2004.

Richter, E.L., Dove, R.W., and Kahl, W. (eds.), *Lehrbuch des katholischen und evangelischen Kirchenrechts*, ed. 8, 1886 (sic!).

Robbers, G. (ed.), *Church autonomy: a comparative survey*, Frankfurt 2001.

Robbers, G., 'Church Autonomy in the European Court of Human Rights—Recent developments in Germany', in *Journal of Law and Religion*, vol. 26, no. 1 (2010–2011).

Robbers, G. (ed.), *State and Church in the EU*, Baden-Baden 2005.

Robbers, G., and W. Cole Durham Jr. (eds.), *Encyclopedia of Law and Religion*, Leiden and Boston 2016.

Rohe, M., *Das islamische Recht. Geschichte und Gegenwart*, C.H. Beck, München 2009.

Rynkowski, M., 'A religious court as a court of a Member State under Article 267 of the TFUE', in: R. Potz, and W. Wieshaider (eds.), *Jurisdictions religieuses et l'Etat*, Granada 2015.

Rynkowski, M., 'Religious Courts in the of the European Court of Human Rights', in *Ecclesiastical Law Journal*, vol. 18, issue 01 (January 2016), pp. 62–66, doi: 10.1017/S0956618X15000848).

Rynkowski, M., *Sądy wyznaniowe we współczesnym europejskim porządku prawnym*, Wrocław 2013.

Sandberg, R., *Law and Religion*, Cambridge 2014.

Sandberg, R., Douglas, G., Doe, N., Gilliat-Ray, S., and Khan, A., 'Britain's Religious Tribunals: 'Joint Governance' in Practice', in: *Journal of Legal Studies*, vol. 33, no. 2 (2013), pp. 263–291, doi: 10.1093/ojls/gqs031.

Settem, O.J., *Application of the "Fair Hearing" Norm in ECHR Article 6(1) to Civil Proceedings, with Special Emphasis on the Balance Between Procedural Safeguards and Efficiency*, Springer, Heidelberg/New York 2016.

Slotte, P., 'The ministerial exception. Theological and legal perspectives from Finland and Europe', in: B.G. Scharffs, A. Maoz, and A. Isaacson Woolley (eds.), *Religious Freedom and the Law: Emerging Contexts for Freedom for and from Religion*, Routledge, Oxford 2018.

Stanisz, P., Zawiślak, M., and Ordon, M. (eds.), *Presence of the Cross in Public Spaces*, Cambridge 2016.

Šturm, L., 'State and Church in Slovenia', in: G. Robbers (ed.), *State and Church in the EU*, Baden-Baden 2005.

Torfs, R., 'The presence of the cross in public spaces from the perspective of the European Court of Human Rights', in: P. Stanisz, M. Zawiślak, and M. Ordon (eds.), *Presence of the Cross in Public Spaces*, Cambridge 2016.

Walter, Ch., *Religionsverfassungsrecht in vergleichender und internationaler Perspektive*, Tübingen 2006.

Warnink, H. (ed.), *Legal position of churches and church autonomy*, Leuven 2001.

Williams, R., 'Civil and Religious Law in England—a Religious Perspective', in: 10 *Ecclesiastical Law Journal* (2008), p. 262.

www.ingramcontent.com/pod-product-compliance
Lightning Source LLC
Chambersburg PA
CBHW031333230926
51848CB00001B/218
9789004416482